Su Teatro: 20 Yea

Selected Plays
by
Anthony J. García

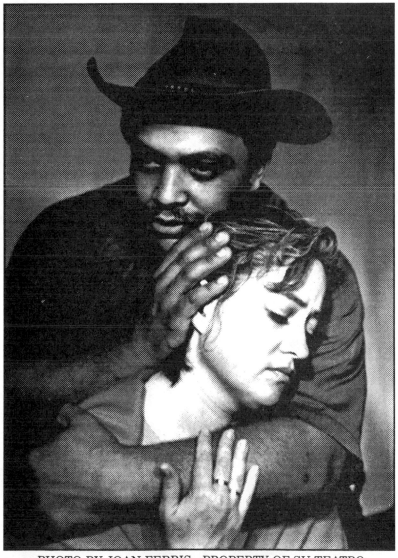

PHOTO BY JOAN FERRIS - PROPERTY OF SU TEATRO
ANGEL MENDEZ-SOTO AND KATHY SALAZAR IN A SCENE FROM
SERAFIN;CANTOS Y LAGRIMAS

Foreword

Su Teatro: 20 year Anthology, is perhaps more of an overview of my participation in the company than an historical compilation. Perhaps, because of our geographical location and because our impact on social and cultural activity has been gradual and not as dramatic as a group such as El Teatro Campesino, there has never been an independent chronicler of Su Teatro. It is therefore left to future El Centro Su Teatro archivists to someday present that perspective.

The Beginnings

When Su Teatro was formed in January of 1971, El Teatro Campesino was already on the cutting edge of the theatrical world. In fact it was after seeing a performance by El Teatro that Rowena Rivera and a handful of others decided to form a class at the University of Colorado at Denver, entitled, "Intro to Chicano Theatre." Some, but not all of the original members were Tep Falcón, Arturo Valdez, Yvonne Sanchez, Rocky Hernandez, Chris Montoya, Dalia Longoria, Carmelita Muníz, Diana DeHerrera and Alícia Lucero.

I joined in June of 1972, I was 19, and a student at UCD and an active member of the United Mexican American Students. Mateo Torres and Carlos Santillanez and I were boyhood friends, who although lacking formal training had all performed at one time or another. Of the three, I was the least talented, Carlos was an accomplished singer and guitarist, and Mateo was an award winning playwright. I sang, played guitar and acted, none of these I did well. Arturo Valdez, in my opinion was the creative leadership, when I joined. Tep and Diana, however were the political and spiritual strength of the group. Alfredo Sandoval became a member of the company at about the same time as Mateo, Carlos and myself. He soon developed into the strongest actor in the company.

Within two years, the company had changed tremendously. In the fall of 1973, I had left the teatro because I was going to school at the University of Colorado in Boulder. Even though it was only 20 miles away, it was a world apart. I returned in the spring of 1974, to find the new teatro members preparing to attend the 5th Annual TENAZ (Teatros Nacíonales de Aztlan) Festivál, it was called El Primer Encuentro Latinoamericano and it was to take place in Mexico City in the Summer of 1974.

In the spring of 1973, I had written a couple of small actos for the company, one was called *Reyes and Raul*, it was about 2 young Chicanos, one male and one female, caught up in a futuristic foxhole of the impending Chicano Revolution. The other was an agit-prop piece written after the death of Luis Jr. Martinez, a young Chicano affiliated with the Crusade for Justice, who was killed in a shoot-out with the Denver Police Department. I do not remember the name of the, "acto" but the intent was to draw attention to the violence of the police. I remember being furious about the piss poor performance of the teatro, and vowing never to write for the teatro again, unless I could direct the piece as well. Su Teatro however was neither ready nor willing to accept direction from its youngest and least talented member.

When I rejoined the company, after returning from Boulder, in the spring of 1974, I began working closely with Alfredo Sandoval who was now directing the company. He was working on an original piece to be performed with the Denver Symphony Orchestra. The DSO would perform Manuel DeFalla's *The Three Cornered Hat* and the teatro would perform in front of the symphony. Needless to say the marriage was a very unhappy union, however it gave me my first opportunity for hands on directing. Prior to that time I had to direct through Alfredo. Although Alfredo was officially the director, who had done a tremendous job in recruiting members and maintaining the teatro, more and more I was being given opportunities to direct - all with Alfredo's encouragement and support.

Before it begins to appear as though everyone was just mean to me, I have to admit that I was not the most pleasant person. For every progressive idea I offered, I was always able to counter with a strong dose of immaturity. None of these worked to solidify my leadership.

It took years to convince some people that I was serious about my work. My actions made it difficult for me to win respect for my work and for Su Teatro. Although in retrospect the talents and efforts of the core group was tremendous, I really believe that the contributions of the members of Su Teatro is the body of work.

La Familia sin Fabiano

After the DSO fiasco, I began working on what would be Su Teatro's first full length play. It was called, *La Familia Sin Fabiano*. The story line centered around the death of the father, Fabiano, and the chain-reaction that occurs throughout the family. The eldest son is an Army veteran, and has become a gung-ho, " American," the middle daughter is married to a Euro-American, who despises Fabiano and all that he represents culturally, and the hero is the youngest Chicano militant son. The father represented Mexico and his Mejicanismo is to be honored, respected and resurrected. It was not a unique message, but one that was being played out in Chicano homes across the country. It also presented themes being duplicated on Chicano stages across the country.

La Familia Sin Fabiano was not a very good play but it featured many of the political and artistic influences prevalent in the Chicano cultural movement. It still was, nonetheless a straight drama. And it represented the highest level of Su Teatro's development. It was the first play I directed. And it also advanced my position as an artistic leader in the company.

After performances in Mexico City at the TENAZ Festivál, the play was rewritten to include all the new ideas to which we had been exposed. Somehow, through a quirk in scheduling, we ended up as the opening act for the "world famous" El Teatro Campesino, and upon returning to Denver, the play began to look a lot like their production of, *La Carpa de los Rasquachis.* . The play now included elements of the mito, agit-prop, social realism, more music to accompany the action and actors moved in and out of character in an unknowing reference to Bertolt Brecht.

After returning from Mexico, many members of the company quit. The experience represented their peak interest in the theatre. What was left was a stronger core of performers, charged up by their experience and dedicated to the advancement of "the cultural arm of the revolutionary struggle", as the TENAZ' (Teatros Nacional de Aztlán the Festivál's sponsoring group) principles of unity read.

In the fall of 1974, the company included Alfredo Sandoval, Paul Marín, Blanca Lucero, Tony Lucero, their daughter Nikki Lucero, Carlos Santillanez, and Benito Montoya - all had been on the trip to Mexico with us. There were two new members who would prove to be the most significant additions to the company.

Yolanda Ortega and Debra Gallegos

Yolanda Ortega, had joined the teatro, prior to the TENAZ Festivál, but too late to be a part of the trip. Yolanda could sing, act, dance and spoke Spanish fluently. This was a valuable asset for a group of third and fourth generation inner-city pochos, only rediscovering their history and language. She had some formal acting training. But mostly, she was an experienced performer. Many of the Colorado teatros, at one time there were ten, were activists becoming performers. Su Teatro consisted of performers becoming activists.

Debra Gallegos was the newest member, she had acted in high school. She played the guitar and along with Yolanda they created a vocal interweaving that made them sound as one. With Carlos, Yolanda, Debra and myself, Su Teatro became a very strong musical company. We have been able to attract other musicians, in particular singers, over the years. That tradition which cohered in 1974, continues to this day.

In 1975, the company began work on the first full length production that would emphasize the newly developed musical strength of Su Teatro. It was to be a story about the neighborhood in the old Westside of Denver, near St. Cajetan's Church. It was where I had grown up and it had been the religious, cultural, and political center of the Chicano community. Without going into the treacherous political mechanizations that led to the depopulation of this community in order to build, what is now called the Auraria Higher Education Center, I will say that the loss was very difficult for the Chicano community.

It was while walking to rehearsal one afternoon that I passed along Ninth St., perhaps the main pedestrian thoroughfare of the neighborhood, that I saw the houses that were boarded up - the ghosts of neighbors, families and friends seemed to call out. Places where I had seen life begin, celebrated and end, now seemed muzzled and pained. I remember going to rehearsal and presenting an idea for the next production.

It would be a "a corrido", which literally is a story put to music, however as presented in teatro Chicano, it was a play put to music. It would become *El Corrido de Auraria*, Auraria being the indigenous name for the neighborhood, which was later being revived by developers. That night we improvised the first scenes, and still struggling with our reborn Spanish, wrote the first verse of the, *El Corrido de Auraria*.

> *Aqui vivmos en el barrio de Westside Denver,*
> *Los vecinos están como campadre,*
> *Trabajamos, lloramos y cantamos,*
> *Porque somos todo lo que tenemos.*

The development of the play took fully a year, and was still evolving, in 1976, when it took a new direction to include anti-United States bicentennial messages. It also incorporated a poem by Abelardo "Lalo" Delgado, one of the chingón poet gods of the Chicano Movement. *El Corrido* represents the establishment of stylistic constants that would become recognized in Su Teatro's work. That being the incorporation of music and action. The music at times served as a Greek chorus, commenting on the action. At times the singing bore no relationship to the themes, thus utilizing the music to counterpoint the themes.

An example of this would be a love song that would backup a particularly violent scene. This concept went back to *La Familia sin Fabiano*, where Johnny the youngest son is being beaten by the police to the strains of a soft folksong. For the first time, in *El Corrido,* thanks to Debra and Yolanda, we had personnel to experiment more in this area. We drew other members who also possessed musical experience, Debora Montoya, James Cortez and Deborah Roybál. *El Corrido* toured Colorado. It was rewritten in 1982 and had a very successful run at the Slightly Off Center theater and included a weekend at the Denver Center for the Performing Arts. Later, it was revived and once again rewritten and then renamed *El Corrido del Barrio*. In 1990, it opened the second season at El Centro Su Teatro.

In 1977, I wanted to move on to create a new work. I had become fascinated with the story of the Ludlow mining strike. Much as this had to do with my increasing working-class consciousness and the discovery that what many thought was a strike that was led by Italians, Russians and other nationalities, also include large participation by the Mexicanos that lived in Southern Colorado where the strike took place.

In fact it was a large number of Mexicanos who were killed in the subsequent massacre that really drew my interest.

The original Ludlow script

It was during this time that the brewery workers went on strike against the Adolph Coors Brewing Company. For those familiar with Coors and the Coors family, you know that they have a long history of antagonism towards workers and are staunchly anti-union. Also, money has been, in my opinion, funneled by Coors into non-profit organizations such as the Heritage Foundation, Mountain States Legal Foundation, the Independence Institute and the Mountains States Employers Council, who have in turn sponsored and supported legislation and actions that have been detrimental for Chicanos. Given this deep seeded conviction, the strike was a tremendous inspiration for the play.

The play was performed in various locations throughout Colorado. However, it often represented the dogmatic and sometimes stilted aesthetics of the political positions the group held during that time. It also represented a transition. Yolanda was not working with us at this time, Debra, who had established herself as the best actor in the company, through *Ludlow*, was leaving. We were anxiously looking for a replacement. Other veterans were moving into marriages and raising families and had less time for the teatro and their replacements did not have the experience or the skills to maintain the level of quality. In 1978, in Boulder *Ludlow; El Grito de las Minas* was performed for the last time., in what would be Debra's last official performance with Su Teatro.

The original production of *Ludlow; El Grito de las Minas* included two new members, Jody Ewing and Sheila Perez, who have continued to be supportive of Su Teatro and its goals.

The Movement in Transition

For nearly two years, from the Spring of 1978 and the winter of 1979, Su Teatro consisted of Sheila Pérez, Verónica Benavidez, myself and anyone else we could get to perform with us. Debra, Yolanda and Jody had banded together to form a musical group, which they called Flor de la Quebrada. They had been influenced by the Nueva Cancíon Movement which was very strong in Chile and other parts of Latin America.

During this time Su Teatro produced collective performances with Flor de la Quebrada and an actual Chilean group known as Los Chasquis (the Messengers). The company was not strong enough to produce work on its own. This was the closest to folding, I can recall Su Teatro ever being. The individuals as well as the company were searching for some source of inspiration in the pre-Reagan, post-revolutionary times.

In looking back, this period confirms what I believe has been what has caused Su Teatro to survive. Every ebb that we had was followed by a period of Su Teatro rebuilding stronger. There were three major ebbs. The first was when Alfredo rebuilt the company after I left for Boulder, in 1974. The next period was when everyone went in different directions in

1978, and in 1983 when the turmoil of our personal lives caused all hell to break loose.

Artistic growth has pulled Su Teatro out of each of its slumps. In 1974, it was the productions of *La Familia sin Fabiano* and *El Corrido del Barrio* that were clearly better works than any that the previous membership had produced.

In 1979, it was the addition of Rudy Bustos, Judy Sandoval and Angel Mendez-Soto, which culminated in the production of *El Corrido de Auraria* at the Slightly Off Center theater in 1982, and the 1984 slump was broken with the addition of Sherry Coca-Candelaria and the return of Debra Gallegos for the production of *Intro to Chicano History: 101* at the Public Theatre in New York City in 1985.

The Funk

The period of 1979 through 1984 was known as ,"the Funk", not because of any tribute to the mindless popular musical trends that included disco, funk and self-absorbed tributes to the cultural wasteland that was taking place throughout the country during this time period. "The Funk", therefore, did not represent some monotonous ass shaking dance experience, it referred to a stifling depressing non-creative period in Su Teatro's history. Little did we realize that the entire country was in the same condition. The country was rushing to the right, some Chicanos were declaring the Movement dead and becoming Hispanics for the sake of their own survival. Such was the winter of Ronald Reaganism.

In the early years, we did not realize that we were in a rut. However, the record of our work indicates that we were. Rudy Bustos joined the company in December of 1979. His addition gave us another musician to the company. He was a singer and guitarist and he understood musical arrangement. He was an objective voice between the musical opinions of Debra, Yolanda, and myself. He helped solidify the musical component, which was all we really were, at that time. A Su Teatro performance in 1980 might include Rudy and myself, Angel on flute, Judy singing with either Debra, Yolanda or Jody, depending on who we conned into performing. True to our, "Everyone can participate" roots, performances also included two 12 year-olds Cindy Lopez and Shawna Daily.

After years of seeing our work as primarily a support mechanism for political issues, and also being told this by our so-called leftist allies, we began to feel the frustration of never developing ourselves as artists. For years we had been called in to keep the rally lively, between the monotony of the more "important" political speeches. Every intellectual could tell you all about the importance of art and culture, but none knew what to do about it. Art and culture were mostly belittled by people who saw it as frivolous, but were willing to use the teatro opportunistically, if it meant drawing people to their events.

There were also two different viewpoints, with in the teatro, about what the teatro should be doing. Some people felt it was best served by being a "living leaflet", if you will, of the movement. They felt it was okay for the company to be producing immediate, although not significant skits. to support an increasingly ungrateful left. We received regular calls to perform at rallies, demonstrations and political events, we mostly performed last to assure that the important speakers were heard first.

There were also those who felt that the cultural work alone was a big enough area of work. I guess it is clear that I was on the second group's side. The final straw came when we found out that these same white leftists that had criticized our political commitment and tried to guilt trip us into countless free performances, were paying large dollars to out of town visiting cultural performers, whom they treated with extreme respect and consideration.

We lost our fear or guilt in asking for money, we also let it be known that we were going into workshop and were available for performances only with advance notice and on a limited basis.

El Corrido del Barrio

The quality of our performances rose, when the company performed, *El Corrido de Auraria* at the Slightly Off Center theater for six weeks. We finally achieved a level of what we had long sought, that being the respect of our community and our political peers. We would never look at ourselves in the old way.

By the end of the run , *El Corrido* was playing to overflow houses, and was clearly being talked about in the Chicano community in a way that was causing the conservative Hispanics sorts to have to deal with us. At this time, unbeknownst to us, there were forces who believed that the cultural movement was best served by presenting a more modified view of the Mexican-American experience. To this end they advanced the position that Su Teatro was too radical and that Tony García was too angry and too difficult to work with, the second part was probably true, but Su Teatro has never been too radical, at least for my tastes. In keeping with this viewpoint, they advanced themselves to the major institutions as viable alternatives to political art. To the contrary *El Corrido de Auraria* which was too preachy for some was invited to be presented at the Denver Center for the Performing Arts. The weekend run in the 400 seat house ran to 3/4 capacity.

The significance of this event was multi-fold, during the Slightly Off Center run, I was not a member of Su Teatro. Feeling that I could not operate under the democratic-collectivism of the then Su Teatro structure (under this structure, the directors casting choices had to be reviewed and approved by the company. I wanted to audition and cast as I saw fit), I requested a leave of absence and paid royalties to produce my own play. As producer-director-author, I was able to make personnel and artistic choices free from the often personal and political pressure of the internal Su Teatro workings.

I asked Debra and Yolanda to serve as producers of the play. They helped with the rewrites, which were significant. Yolanda used many of her contacts to provide audition space and tons of community outreach. Being well known and respected in the community, as well as in professional circles, Yolanda proved a bridge to people that I could only piss off. Steve Munro a local theatrical director and producer, spent hours talking to me about the ins and outs of theater producing. He actually took me by the hand and introduced me to the local theater media. The coverage by the press was tremendous, it was unheard of for a company such as ours to be getting so much attention, while our business and political leaders ignored us.

Mark Gitlis, who ran the Slightly Off Center theater (which was called slightly off center, because the stage was slightly off center from the audience) allowed me to be immediately inserted into his season and to direct a play, with a script he had never seen, until he joined the cast for the second production. Roy Crawford, was the house technical director at SOC, he also joined us for the Denver Center run. He would be with us 4 years later in New York for *Intro to Chicano History:101*.

The SOC run gave me access to people with greater theatrical experience, as well as teaching, I was learning. From technical language to theatrical norms, this was a unique experience for all of us. For the first time I was making financial and artistic decisions, and growing more confident in my ability to do so. *El Corrido de Auraria* made money, the actors got paid a small stipend. I made money and we made an impact. *El Corrido* had brought Chicanos, many seeing theater for the first time, to see a play about themselves. And they were willing to pay the five dollar cover, for this experience. It contradicted the mainstreamers, who felt that political theater was passé and that we needed the dominant culture to legitimize ourselves. *El Corrido* proved that we could succeed on our own.

I left the teatro after *El Corrido* at the Slightly Off Center, feeling that the demands of the company were causing too much strain on my marriage. (But perhaps, secretly feeling that the marriage was putting too much of a demand on my teatro). When the offer to perform at the DCPA arrived, Su Teatro hired Dutch Shindler to act as producer, and me to direct. While the show produced large audiences, primarily Chicano, we had begun to add loyal followers of white political types and theatre-goers, nonetheless, the production lost money.

The lessons I learned confirmed some things that I had known and corrected some things that I thought I knew. It reinforced my suspicions about large Euro-American institutions, even art institutions. It proved that there was a uniqueness and a high quality to our work. I began for the first time to see myself as a playwright. It proved that the dominant culture could not give me legitimacy, no matter how much you may try to appease them. It also established Su Teatro as a much broader force in the Chicano community. This is what I knew, what I did not understand was that there was an even bigger need for what we were doing. That we were not in fact an isolated voice in the shadow of the Reagan years, but instead there existed others like us. And, also that Su Teatro could no longer work as a collective, in every aspect. If I was to direct, I had to make casting and artistic choices.

Rudy Bustos emerged from *El Corrido* as an administrative leader. He arranged bookings to retire the debt to the Denver Center. He, along with Judy Sandoval, moved to incorporate the organization legally within the state of Colorado. Also, after taking over the lead in *El Corrido*, he began to act more. He helped to keep the company functioning. He also provided artistic direction in guiding the music. Even though, all my Latin American influenced songs began to have a New Mexican garage band feel to them, the company was now charged up to perform.

I had left the company with no plan to return. I had been unemployed off and on, going through a variety of jobs. I also had family issues as my older sister was dying from a brain tumor. I was drinking heavily and felt as though I was pretty much on my own.

Serafin: Cantos y Lagrimas

During this time the diaries of my father began to haunt me. After his death, my sister Rachel had given me a calendar, that he had used as a diary. On days when he was drinking, he wrote D. When he would stop he would write, " Today I didn't. Couldn't get out of bed. Threw up." For the second day, "Stayed in bed, threw up a little, couldn't eat."

What I realized was that, alcohol had become the center of his life, before himself, before his family and before his. He was bent on self-destruction. I understood that I was harboring the same artist fantasies, "live fast, die young and leave a good looking corpse." I wanted to explore that darkness, in which my father lived. As I had been a part of it, when I was drunk, and obviously couldn't figure a damn thing out.

I spent time studying drunks, which today we would call street people. I seldom spoke to them because to learn I had to listen. I spent a few all nighters hanging out, near the warehouses and under the bridges.

When the time came to write *Serafin: Cantos y Lagrimas* it took me all of 53 hours. I wrote for two days straight, on a very ineffective typewriter, that my ex-wife had given me. I worked straight only taking breaks to eat, stretch and move away from the deep pain this character carried. I began at 10 P.M. Friday night and finished at around 5 on Sunday morning. It was as though I had journeyed a lifetime in a weekend. I had passed through my father's life and into mine. I rousted the people I loved, and shared the script. Even in its raw form, we all realized that *Serafin: Cantos y Lagrimas* was a deeper and stronger work than any I had previously produced. It was also the first script I had completed alone, without the teatro's help.

Although, I remember Angel and Sherry being in the room, while I was writing Luisito's death scene. We took a break, because we knew that Serafin's son would die in the next few words. While Angel went to the bathroom and Sherry went into the kitchen, I returned to the typewriter and completed the scene. When they came back into the room, the deed was done, Luisito was dead.

Years later, when my daughter would accept on my behalf the local critic's award for Best New Play or some shit like that, she would say that, even though she never knew Símon García her grandfather, perhaps, *Serafin* was giving her back her father. I often think that maybe my father's gift to me was this play that made believe I was a writer.

Serafin... was completed in the summer of 1985, it was performed at the First Annual Summer Showcase at the Changing Scene Theatre. It was while carrying set pieces and platforms up the stairs at 2 o'clock on a Sunday morning that I realized that Su Teatro needed its own home. The revelation actually came to me in the realization that I was too old to carry this shit.

However, before we could follow up the successful workshop of *Serafin: Cantos y Lagrimas* and move into our own building, *Intro to Chicano History:101* happened. In the ten months since I stopped drinking, I had written 3 plays *Serafin...*, a mediocre piece called *And the Worm Turns* and the last play was a musical-historical overview of 450-plus years since the conquest of the New World, *Intro to Chicano History: 101*.

I had been developing the play for sometime but had never attempted to produce it, because the personnel in the company were not strong enough musically. But when Su Teatro was invited to perform at the Latino Theater Festival, at the Public Theater in New York City that much changed. This cast included myself, Rudy, Sherry, and Angel. Debra Gallegos and Alfredo Sandoval were added to speed the development of the show. My daughter, Micaela was written into the play, so she could make the trip to New York.

Additionally a longtime friend of mine Jaime Gomez, a playwright, director, musician and performer was brought in to help me. Jaime who writes under the name Armando Carnal, allowed us to use his song *La Gran Gente del Sol (Gente Valiente)* and introduced the character of the Vato Loco as the protagonist in the play. After New York, *Intro* developed a life of its' own, with extended runs at the Little Theatre at Denver University and much later at El Centro Su Teatro. The play also traveled the Southwest and Mexico, logging well over 200 performances.

Due to the overwhelming success of *Intro to Chicano History:101* everything was placed on the back burner until, 1987, when the company reorganized itself for the purchase of the building. I had grown weary of traveling and scrambling for space. The plan was very simple, we would purchase a building in the barrio. We would perform plays I had written, everyone would come and life would be so easy.

El Centro Su Teatro

Everyday on my way from picking up my daughter at day care, Micaela would point to the Elyria Elementary School building and say "that gonna be my school. Huh Dad?" The school had been closed for a couple of years, and the talk was that it would soon be used as a pre-school and day care center. I looked forward to the day I wouldn't have to drive her across town to another daycare center. Years later, storyteller Jerry Lawson, knowing that I was looking for a home for the theater, suggested the Elyria School building. I remember telling her how wrong it was, and that she should really mind her own business, as I knew what was best for Su Teatro. She insisted, so I asked Debra to see what she could find out.

It turns out that the building had been vacant, and since my daughter was now in middle school, time had pretty much run out on that pre-school idea, at least for me it had. Jerry García, who worked for the Community Development Agency for the city was actually responsible for the building. Jerry was an old acquaintance of the teatro, and had helped Su Teatro in its first attempt to establish a centro when he was the director of the Denver Inner City Parish. It seems that getting this building was in fact, a very real possibility.

The drive to establish El Centro Su Teatro benefited from two external factors, one was the collapse of the local real estate market thanks to Neil Bush and his cronies in the Savings and Loan fiasco, and the other was the establishment of the Scientific and Cultural Facilities District and the arts tax that went with it. Although the vast majority of the money went to support the major (established Euro-centric) arts centers, some of money actually trickled down to community based arts centers of color.

The Elyria Elementary School building was acquired on my birthday in April, I remember Debra calling me at the print shop where I was working to wish me a happy birthday. I was immediately suspicious, because it was the first time in the 12 years I had known Debra that she had called me at work to recognize my birthday. She then told me that she had gotten a call from Jerry García telling her that the building was ours.

El Centro Su Teatro opened on May 12, 1989. It was to become the precipice of a long time vision of the founding and core members of the company. At the opening ceremony, Grupo Tlalóc consecrated the grounds, Bill High and Sonora Catering provided the dinner, and the company performed *Intro to Chicano History:101,* for the first time in it's own home, in the classroom that would someday serve as administrative offices.

It would also become home to my work, it presented an opportunity of a lifetime to me. I had a company of actors, a theater in which to work and peers, who had established a sharp understanding of my artistic vision and were keen in their ability to criticize and correct my work.

In the Fall of 1989, we opened the season with *Serafin: Cantos y Lagrimas,* because of the success of *Intro,* we had not had the opportunity to produce *Serafin,* which became a tremendous success, running for three months in the newly renovated theater space. Over the years, El Centro was the home for the world premier of *Ludlow; El Grito de las Minas* and *The Day Ricardo Falcón Died.*

Both plays had earlier beginnings, *Ludlow,* was completely re-worked, except for the title and the opening song it was a new play. *Ricardo Falcón* came to because of a clause in the Chicano Playwrighting contest, a national contest originating out of the University of California at Irvine. Having won the award for playwriting previously, I was no longer eligible in that category, so I was encouraging others to apply. On a bet with a friend, I agreed to write a short story to match hers and we would then submit them together. Neither of us won, but I liked my story enough to write a first act and call it a play.

I wrote *Obsidian Rain,* while I was in San Antonio, working on *El Milagro* a play by acclaimed Mexican director Felipe Santander. I had heard about the strip mining being done in San Luis and about the chemicals being used to extract gold from the mountains, and in the process poisoning the water, and I wanted to make a statement about it. *Little Hands Hold the Wind* was commissioned by Ruby Nelda Perez, as a one person show. The play has not seen the light of day as a production, but was produced as an audio-drama cassette. The problem with an audio-drama is that not only do people not read anymore, they flat out can't listen. I present *Little Hands...* to you because I think it is a good story, and has something to say.

In reading this Anthology, you will find the path of a "Generation's Journey", one that began as teenagers, and continues into middle age. Su Teatro is the third oldest Chicano Theater company that has operated continuously since inception. It has offered its work as a cultural and artistic commitment to its community and the country. As you turn the pages it is not only my words that you will be reading, it will be my words channeled through the creative spirits and relayed through the interpretations of Debra, Yolanda, Rudy, Angel, Sherry, Manuel, Alfredo and the other members of the company, of which I am proud to say, that I am but one.

Su Teatro 20 Years Anthology
Selected plays by Anthony J. García

This book is dedicated to Debra and Yolanda, who have given so much to me and have worked to establish and maintain high artistic standards for the company and whose dedication has inspired Su Teatro's strong commitment to the community.

It is also dedicated to my daughter Micaela, who is everything to me, to my mother Mollie Chavez, who is the true master storyteller and to Millie Duran, who gives me strength and love.

Table of Contents

Serafin; Cantos y Lagrimas
Serafin; (Songs and Tears)

Picture from Serafin; cantos y lagrimas

Riveting

'Serafin' is a sweeping tragicomedy of a life on the edge, on the ropes

y MIKE PEARSON
cky Mountain News Staff Writer

Distilled to its essence, effec-
e theater is truth — not pan-
amic sets or extravagant cos-
mes, but rich, resonant ideas
d images.

And yet, truth isn't a commod-
y that large theater companies
en celebrate. True, they dust
f a Eugene O'Neill play here or

Review

Edward Albee piece there,
en filter it through enough ex-
nsive trappings, making it pal-
able instead of powerful.

Not so with El Centro Su Tea-
o, which can't afford gilded
ckaging and thus delivers un-
dorned theater with uncompro-
ising guts. Anthony J. Garcia's
rafin: Cantos y Lagrimas
ongs and Tears) proves that the
ger of realism can purify and
ll entertain.

After 15 years as an actor
aywright with Su Teatro, Gar-
a knows how to disarm an audi-
ce. Serafin is a sweeping tragi-
medy about life — life on the
ge, on the ropes, in the dumps,
the bottle and in transition.
s also about families, lost
ildhood and the sheer inso-
ce of memory.

To pack all these elements into
mere 85 minutes is no simple
t. But Garcia isn't a simple

Serafin: Cantos y Lagrimas

A play by Anthony J. Garcia presented by El Centro Su Teatro, 4725 High
St. Directed by Anthony Garcia, with
Serafin, Angel Mendez-Soto; Lucio/
Don Peion, Gabriel J. Guereca; Maria-
luisa/Rafaela, Kathy Salazar. Performances 8 p.m. Thursdays through
Saturdays, through November. 296-
0219.

playwright. He blends the ethnic
defiance of Luis Valdez with the
social crusading of Sinclair Lew-
is and the haunting memory-play
device of Tennessee Williams to
cover a lot of ground in a short
time.

The play opens with the main
character, a 60-something bum
named Serafin, collapsing in a
dark alley, whiskey and ciga-
rettes on his breath. The audience is like the priest in confessional, anonymously attending as
Serafin lies wounded from a
mugging and relives his life in
words.

And what words they are.
Combined with Angel Mendez-
Soto's remarkable acting, those
words paint a picture of life as a
young child in revolutionary
Mexico, where his father disappears into Pancho Villa's army.
Later, after his mother's death,
9-year-old Serafin takes his
brother and sister and flees to
the United States, finding work
in a farmer's field.

As the years melt away, we
find Serafin as a union organizer
in Greeley, a family man in Den-

ver and, finally, a nomad shorn
of wife and children, lost in time
on the lonely streets. The Serafin
who weaves this tale is a court
jester willing to perform for the
cost of a bottle. His journey,
from hope to despair to fatalistic
acceptance, is the driving force
of this play.

Despite such peripheral characters as Serafin's sister-turned-
opera-star (Kathy Salazar) and
his brother Lucio, spiritually destroyed during the Bataan death
march, Garcia's play is a one-
character monologue. Mendez-
Soto interacts mainly with offstage voices — voices that recall
people and places in his life and
serve as surrealistic markers for
viewers. Factor in a script that
mingles Spanish and English to
great advantage and you have a
powerful tale.

One could find fault with Garcia's occasionally erratic stag-
ing, but what would be the point?
Ultimately the triumph of this
production is not in how it is
directed, but how it is acted and
written. The writing is uniformly
strong, and Mendez-Soto's performance does justice to every
word. You believe his pain and
anguish, just as you delight in the
sparkle that flashes in the eyes of
a character at peace with his
failings.

From the moment Mendez-
Soto stumbles drunkenly onto the
stage, Serafin and the audience
become one.

Program notes:
September 1989

There is a time when we all face an innerself that torments us.

In this sense, *Serafín* is a very individual story, a story about choices we must face. Yet, there is more because these choices concern family, history and pride. *Serafín* is a man, not unlike my father, strong and caring, but at what point did the bottle take control?

Serafín is a witness to history, to triumph and defeat. We must travel with him, for his is a journey that has been taken by our parents, a journey that led them to us.

Serafín was written in two days in 1984. It was written with much support from loved ones. Even with such support, there were times when I had to leave the room, walk away from the typewriter. I had to take a break from the complexity, which is this man-Serafín.

I have waited five years to direct this piece. It took seventeen years for Su Teatro to find a home. Now Serafín's voice will find an audience to be heard.

Serafin; Cantos y Lagrimas
Serafin; (Songs and Tears)

Written & Directed by Anthony J. Garcia
Assistant Director by Rodolfo W. Bustos
Technical Director-Leo Griep-Ruiz

Original Cast

Serafin	Angel Mendez-Soto
Lucio/Don Pelón	Gabríel J. Guereca
Marialuisa/Rafael	Kathy Salazar
Musician/Punk #2	Manuel Roybal
Musician/Punk #1	Leo Griep-Ruiz
Musician/Punk #3	Daniel Pedraza
Luisito	Manuel Roybal Jr.
Serafin (Understudy)	Manuel Roybal

Cast of Characters

Serafín	An old drunk in his late sixties.
Marialuisa	Serafín's wife, ten years younger.
Lucio	Serafín's brother, mid forties
Luisito	Serafín's son, fifteen
Sebastían	Union organizer, thirty-five
Rafaela	Serafin's sister, younger than Lucio
Carlos	Serafin's son
Rosalia	Serafin's daughter
Felipe	Serafin's youngest son
Gavacho Farmer	Gavacho farmer
Don Pelón	Owner of the ranchito in Mexico
Punks # 1,2 & 3	

In the present, Serafín is an old drunk. He is seven years old during the time of Pancho Villa's revolution. At the time of the action he is in his late sixties. He is now an alcoholic and has lived on the streets of Denver for several years. He was once a field worker and a union organizer. His body is strong, and in moments he is a powerful man however it is his will that is broken. All other characters are incidental and appear as off-stage voices except for Lucio and Marialuisa. The characters' stage appearances are left to the discretion of the director. The same holds true for the slide show outlined in appendix A.

Scene 1

(From the rear of the theatre a noise is heard. It is a drunken old man, Serafín. He approaches the audience, grumbling obscenities and being rude and obnoxious. After general harassing, he focuses in on someone to bum a cigarette. He demands that it be a menthol cigarette at which point he breaks off the cigarette filter and lights it. He hits stage, the flickering neon light of the skid row bar illuminates the small opening between the bar's outside wall and an old warehouse. It is to this spot that Serafín moves. With his back to the audience he begins to urinate. He is lost in the act of relieving himself. He sings with no particular melody line but in ranchera style.)

Serafín

Yo tomo porque yo quiero, y yo quiero porque yo tomo...

(Behind him four young punks emerge.)

Punk # 1

Hey old man, whatcha think you're doing?

(This startles Serafín, who turns suddenly and sprays everything in sight.)

12

Punk #2

Hey! Watch it with that thing.

Punk #3

Yeah, you're gonna hurt someone.

Serafín

Que quieren?

Punk #1

Hear that? He's a Mexican.

Punk #2

That don't matter. We're in America. Talk to me in English.

(Serafín is defiant. He spits in the direction of the punk, however he misses him. He then swings at him, his swing also misses the punk. The punk beats on Serafín until he collapses.)

Punk # 3

Come on old man talk to me in English. What's the matter, don't you know any?

Punk #1

Come on old man say something.

Punk #2

I can't hear you. **(He sees that Serafín is ready to talk. He leans forward.)** What? **(He leans further in.)** You want to say something now, okay now say it to me in English. **(He puts his ear to Serafín's mouth.)**

13

Serafín

Fuck you.

Punk #2

You old son-of-a-bitch. I'll kill your crazy ass. **(He starts to kick him again and again. The others join in.)**

Punk #1

Okay, okay , let's split. It's too cold to piss around with this old fart.

Punk #2

Yeah, you old bastard you can stay out here all night and freeze to death.

Punk #3

Who cares? It's just an old drunk. He's better off dead.

Punk #1

Let's book. Nobody will even notice he's gone.

(They exit laughing.)

Scene 2

(Music plays, " Cantos y Lagrimas " Appendix B. A voice calls out.)

Papá

Serafin, levantate huevon, ya son las seis de la mañana, **(To himself)** y este huevon esta dormiendo. **(To Serafín)** Fino traigas tus nalgas aqui. Ándale.

Serafín

No Papá, por favór, un ratito mas, ok, bueno. Hay voy.
(He continues to sleep.)

Mamá

Serafin, ándale hito, tu papa necesita tu ayuda. Apurate m'ijo.

Serafín

Si Mamá, yo voy. **(His eyes are still closed)** Dónde están mis
calzones? Mi camisa?

Papá

Aye que cabrón, huevon, donde estás? Voy a agarrarte por tu pelo...

Serafín

(Jumps up quickly, searching for his pants and shirt.) Aqui estoy
Papa, estoy listo. **(He wakes up realizing that he is drunk.)**
Chihuahua! **(He falls back down.)** Mil noviciento y once
(sarcastically.) Papa estoy listo. Why did you have me get dressed?
You were only going to leave? **(He shouts.)** Que viva la revolucíon de
Generalisimo Francisco Villa. **(He answers.)** Que todos se comen
mierda. **(He prays.)** Perdóname. In my pueblito outside of Durango,
we prayed to el poderoso San Villa. Porque his armies were everywhere
and if you didn't fight for Villa, los federales te agaraban por el
ejercito......Mi papa era un hombre muy inteligente, **(Because he is
drunk he has trouble pronouncing the word, finally he spits
out.)** Era muy smart el fregón. He knew that should the federales find
you on your ranchito, they would think you were fighting for the
revolutionaries at night instead of sleeping, I guess? Then they would
hang you or take you off to fight in the government's armies. And if the
federales didn't find you at the ranchito, they would think you were
fighting for the Villistas during the day and sleeping at night. Si esto lo
pasaba, then they would just rape su esposa and burn your ranchito. **(He
speaks as a little boy.)** Papá, porque fuiste ir? Si Papá, I will be the
man of the house. Pero tengo miedo, Papá. Papá a donde va? Cuando
you are in the Los Estados Unidos, will you send for us?

15

No? Will you come back to us? Si Papá, I will take care of the ranchito y Mamá and the niños tambíen. Adios Papá, you will think of us?

Scene 3

Serafín

We called our patron, Don Pelón, porque no tenia cabello. He was fat and puro Español. Era muy feo como Porfirio Diaz pero you would never laugh at Diaz. Don Pelón belonged in Madríd, not in Durango.

Don Pelón

Señora Lozano, donde está su esposo? Micaela por favor contestame. You know I won't hurt him.

Serafín

My Mamá told him que, he left por los Estados Unidos.

Don Pelón

Well Serafín, then you are the man now. Can you tell me where your papá went?

Serafín

(Speaking as a little boy.) Bueno Don Pelón, I mean Don Patrón, es como dice mi Mama. He went to the United Estates.

Don Pelón

Sabes bién que esta es mi tierra. My father let your father work this land and live on it. And what do we get? A few papas and some maiz that your papa manages to grow when he's not off joining revolutionaries to fight against me. You still won't tell me, huh?

16

Serafín

(Speaks as himself.) I don't know what it is about patrones, but the more you tell them the truth the more they think you are lying. So I guess it is better to lie. (Speaks as a boy) Patrón, it is true what you say.

My papá did go off to fight with the Villistas, two weeks ago. (He thinks.) But he fell off his horse in the mountains and broke his neck. He's dead Don Patron. (He begins exaggerated cry.) Papa está muerto.

(Offstage the other children's voices have joined him in crying.)

Don Pelón

Callanse todos. Aye Dios que pena.

Serafín

As we stood pretending to cry, a rider came up to tell Don Pelón that they had found Papá's body. He had been killed trying to outrun the Federales. (Serafin struggles to regain his composure)

Don Pelón

Since our arrangement was between my father and your father, and they are both dead, we have no arrangement. Señora Lozano, you and your family must leave my land. Now, being that I am a Catholic gentleman, I will not leave you to the mercy of my men. But you must leave my land.

Serafín

As he finished talking we heard a shot. It was a sniper. The patrón was dead. His men turned their horses and headed back to the Patrón's hacienda. Later, I found that they had taken everything of value. They burned the hacienda to the ground, then they raped his wife, his daughters and the rest of the women and murdered everyone on the ranchito. Somehow, I never felt sorry for Don Pelón.

I could see his bald head, a big hole in it. His eyes open, looking up at me, he seemed to be saying, "What the hell am I doing here?". We buried him. We would only hope that someone would do the same with Papá's body.

We lived alone on the ranchito and no one bothered us. En tres meces, it would be my eighth birthday, pero I wouldn't spend my birthday on the ranchito. The shack we lived in caught fire, the roof caved in and buried Mamá y Luicito, el mas joven. When my birthday came I was an orphan. Yo y mi hermano Lucio, que tenia seis años, y mi hermanita Rafaelita. Ella tenia cinco años. Fuimos a vivir con los padres de la iglesia Catolica. In the mission there were Franciscans who ate a lot and hated Villa, porque he killed priests. They made us work and pray, all the time work and pray. Yo pensaba, que cuando El Dios venia a salvarnos, no habia nada para salvar.

Yo no me gustaba a ellos y fui a vivir en el ranchito solo. For ten months I hid out on the ranchito. I slept in the establo. I killed rabbit and other small game to survive. I fished and I grew stronger, but mostly I grew angry. On winter nights, I would sneak down to the mission, where Lucio and Rafaela would hide food for me, and the three of us would cry ourselves to sleep. On one of those nights, I took the two of them and we went north, al fin to the United Estates. En Nuevo Mexico, hay mucha gente mejicana, pero ellos creian que eran Españoles. Yo pensaba que eran locos. Los Nuevo Mexicanos se me parecen que eran puro gachupines, pero tenian mucho de la sangre de los indios malos del suroeste. Bueno pues they didn't want to have anything to do with a suromato.

Scene 4

Gavacho Farmer

Bernice, quick come see. Lookee what I found hiding in the barn. Would you shake a leg Bernice. It's a Mexican boy. Well, don't that beat all? And lookee here, he's got a brother and a Mexican girl, too. She's a cute young thing. Easy partner, I ain't a gonna hurt you. Bernice, you reckon the brown hen is the one that laid these three?

Serafín

(Speaking as a boy) No hacemos nada Señor Gavacho. Ya nos vamos. Por favor dejanos pasar.

Gavacho Farmer

Bernice, you know any Mexican? You reckon he wants something?

Serafín

Por favor nomas dejanos ir. **(Serafín speaks as himself)** He moved toward me, pero his wife stopped him. She saw we were hungry and scared. Mi Rafaelita was crying. The gavacho took us in, pero not for free. It was early spring and we helped him with the planting. La lechuga, la papa y el maiz. Y en un rincón chiquitito, sembrarnos chile.

That summer we worked with the farmer and his wife Bernice. Lucio and I slept in the barn. Rafaela, because she was younger, had a bed in the farmer's house which she spread every night and packed away every morning. One night the farmer came to me.

Gavacho Farmer

Fino, you ever see a picture of my boy? This is Billy. I guess he's Bill, now that he's a soldier. He's off fighting in France. Funny, you would think there was enough to fight about back home. It wasn't four years ago, Billy was your age. He helped me plant and seed. Some nights, I come out and look at the stars and when I see the moon and I wonder if it's the same moon he sees at night. When he was a boy he would tell me that the crescent moon up there was his. Do you think he sees it? His Mama prays for him to return. I don't know much about that God stuff, but if it works I'm all for it. I miss him something awful. Ahh, what do you care? All you know is work.

Serafín

Pero, I did know what he was talking about, but it doesn't matter now. I was like a son to the gavacho, sometimes. But mostly I was a field hand. We stayed that summer and longer with the farmer and his esposa, in the fall when we harvested the crop.

Even the chile turned out muy sabroso. We stayed another summer and a fall.

Scene 5

Serafín

Pero, in the spring, Lucio and I moved north, muy norte, hasta Nebraska. Chihuahua! Estabamos con los cornhuskers. We rode un tren into town. No era first class, pero cheap, era gratis. We rode the rails under the train. Verdád. Late one night, Lucio and I snuck into the train yard and found a train facing para el norte y aggaramos. Era nuestra buena suerte que está llegando para el norte.

Híjole, we traveled with the wind blowing through our hair y mucho mas blowing por el otro lado. Te digo, it was a once in a lifetime trip. In Grand Island, Nebraska, habia muchos Mejicanos como yo.

Que estaban haciendo alla? No se. Bueno si se, andaba mucho trabajo en los files. Lucio and I found work as scoopers. Esto es lo que se llamaban, se me hace...que mira, what we did was run behind the truck and gather the corn that had fallen. In Grand Island hay mucho de la cultura mejicana. Habia la comida, el linguaje, muchos bailes y muchas muchachitas mejicanas. **(Music comes up softly in background. The song is a traditional waltz. Serafín makes eyes like he is shy, then he is flirting, then he is shy.)** Muy buenas noches señorita, que linda noche que no? **(He laughs uncomfortably.)** O este hombre es su papa? Serafín Lozano a sus ordenes, señor. **(Serafín, indicates he would like to dance with the daughter.)**

Con su permiso, señor? **(Pause.)** No? Huh? O no, "con su permiso". O si señor, gracias, muchos gracias señor, mil gracias. **(He laughs loudly to himself.)**

It was the first time in my life I ever danced in public. I kept thinking uno, dos, tres, cuatro. **(He laughs even louder, now caught up in the moment.)** Pero, I danced and I married Marialuisa. **(Pause.)** There was a man, his name was Sebastían, who spoke that night at the dance. He was a strong man and many of the men feared him. Many would not look at him, pero they all respected him.

Sebastían

Señores y señoras, yo traigo un mensaje de otros trabajadores de los files. El dia va a venir, que va a existir un sindicato para nosotros.   Un dia vamos a tener el respeto de nuestros derechos como hermanos y como labradores.

El dia está muy cerca, no está tan lejos como se parece.   Hermanos, obreros toman su vida y agarran su futuro.

Serafín

After he spoke everything was very quiet, then the orquestra began to play.   It was like nothing had happened.   The women went back to talking and the men went back to drinking.   Sebastían went through the crowd shaking hands and talking to the men.   Some spoke to him, many would not. (Pause)

Lucio told me to stay away from him.   Some of the men had said that Sebastían was nothing but trouble, maybe even a Communist.   Many of the men did not want trouble.   The cornhuskers were friendly enough, as long as you kept your place.   For someone like Sebastían, there were men who wore white robes and hoods, watching him.

Scene 6

Serafín

Yo vie ha visto a Sebastían, the next week in the fields. I watched him. His eyes were black and his hands were hard.   He stood straight and always spoke in the same sure voice.   I began to follow him from place to place, to hear him speak and watch him with the people.   I followed him to watch, to learn.   No estaba buscando un Cristo pero estaba buscando consejo.   Soon there were others also following him.   We helped him carry his books.   We helped him set up chairs for his meetings.   We listened to him talk about workers in the East, in Europe and the rest of the world.   He said that someday there would be a union for laborers, for Mejicanos in the United Estates.   He said that there might be more.   Some said he might mean Russia. Sebastían, never said.

I never spoke. I was afraid. Tenia miedo que, he might notice that I wasn't very smart and I wasn't very strong, so I never said anything. Pero one day I found out that I wasn't the only one who was following Sebastían. The bosses with the hoods found him one night.

The next morning Lucio and I cut him down from a tree. Lucio, Marialuisa and I were the only ones who were there when they buried him. **(Pause.)** We packed the belongings we had and went back to Nuevo Mexico for Rafaela.

Scene 7

Serafín

When we got there she was gone. Las hermanas en la escuela donde la dejemos sent her to a school para aprender como cantar la opera.

Mother Superior

She has a fine voice Serafín. It is a gift from God. She must share it with the world.

Serafín

Bueno, we will come back for her, when it is our turn to share the gift.

Scene 8

Serafín

Otra vez, nos fuimos para el norte, hasta Colorado, me oi que hay trabajo en las canerias, alla en Greeley. Mucha gente estaba trabajando con las betebeles, yo estaba en la caneria, the canneries. It wasn't long that we had worked, when the first accident happened. The sugar beets were being loaded into one of the railroad cars, when a cable snapped, killing one of the handlers. He was white, pero he was a worker. Within a year, four more were killed, three were Mejicanos.

Two men lost their hands. It was during this time that my first hijo, Luisito was born. It was during this time that we began talking about organizing ourselves for better safety and of course, mas dinero. Yo soy un hombre que en todo su vida no pudria a caller su hocico. I found that it was I who began talking more at meetings and standing up to the bosses. Marialuisa did not try to stop me and Lucio no mas pensaba que yo era un pendejo. All this time, I would see Sebastían's face as the rope hung around his neck. His eyes staring straight ahead and his tongue was sticking out. Remembering the smell made me sick. Pero, still I could hear his voice strong and steady talking about the future we could have.

During this time tuvimos dos niños mas, una niña y un niño. There were many jobs, but soon the bosses did not want to hire me. They said, I had a bad temper. Bueno eso es posible. Pero la gente Mejicana nos conocia y nos respetaba.

En mil noviciento treinta y ocho. Mi hermano, Lucio, fue a ejercito de los Estados Unidos. In 1941, the United Estates went to war. Lucio was in the Far East. He was in the Philippines. He was in Bataan.

(Pause.)

Y aqui the bosses needed bodies. They put everybody back to work. They even brought more Mejicanos into the country, they even made some of us supervisors. At first the Mejicanos that were promoted were a relief from the gavachos, they replaced. **(To supervisor.)** Mira Joaquin, esta escalera ya no sirve. No vale pinche mierda.

Joaquin

Listen, I don't care how you do it, just get it done. And call me Jake.

Serafín

Mira Jake, if one of us climbs up on that ladder vamos a caernos y quebrarnos a nuestras nalgas.

Joaquin

Look Serafín, if you don't want to work here, esta suave. Pero Mexicans are a dime a dozen.

If you don't want the job, get out of the way so those of us that do want to work, can.

Serafín

(Dropping the ladder at his feet.) Orale Joaquin, por cuanto te vendistes? **(Pause.)** That day I collected my last paycheck.

(Turns to take a drink of the bottle of wine.)

Scene 9

Serafín

We stayed in Greeley the rest of the summer. I found odd jobs and Marialuisa took a part-time job bookkeeping for one of the local contractors.

Pero, that fall mi hijo mayor, Luisito, quit school to join the harvesters. He went to work to help the family, porque his Papá couldn't work.

Contractor

Serafín, we would like to hire you pero, you're too old, and besides the Patrón doesn't want any trouble.

Serafín

(Serafín turns away, contractor no longer exists.) Look at my hands, see the cuts, see how flat my fingers are and the bones, when it gets cold, the bones make it hard to move my hands. **(Serafín indicates the various scars and deformities on his hands.)** This is from the fields, this is from picking beets, this is from cutting them and smashing my hands from loading them and now you tell me that I am too old, que ya no sirve. **(Serafín picks up his bottle, takes a long drink and returns to a state of drunkenness only to be brought out by the voice of his son Luisito.)**

Luisito

Papá, que está haciendo aqui? I mean, you never come out to the fields.

24

Serafín

Toma este poncho.

Luisito

Porque Papá, no está lluviendo?

Serafín

Your Mamá had me bring it. **(Uncomfortable being in the work place.)** Toma, you know how she is. **(Looks to the sky.)** She saw the clouds. **(Luisito is still not convinced.)** That's what I thought too, pero you know, I was just sitting around the house. Toma esto tambíen. **(He hands him a taco.)** I was making myself something to eat anyway. **(They begin to eat.)** You wanting to work with the harvesters, is a very big choice, hijo. It's good for you to help the family, pero you have to think of yourself tambíen.

Luisito

I know Papá, pero sometimes, I think its important that we do things right now. I am young, I have plenty of time, but the family must eat today.

Serafín

Mira, ya viene la llúvia. Estás listo para ir? **(They begin to walk down the road.)**

Luisito

Papá, when you were younger, did you try to save the world?

Serafín

No hijo, I couldn't even save my money. Porque dices eso.

Luisito

Some of the men in the fields found out I was your hijo, and they asked me if I wanted to save the world too.

Serafín

Well do you?

Luisito

I don't know what I would do with the world once I saved it.

Serafín

So that means no?

Luisito

No.

Serafín

So that means yes?

Luisito

No.

Serafín

So which one is it?

Luisito

I don't think about it. I know that there is something better in life, but I don't know what it is. This is all I've ever known and all I know is that we have to keep on going.

26

Serafín

We better keep going because we still have a long way home.

Luisito

Papá, did you try to save the world?

Serafín

Can't you tell I was such a big success? **(Returns to acting as the narrator.)** Marialuisa was right about the clouds. The rain was now pouring as if a seam had ripped in the sky. A truck pulled up behind us. It was filled with hay. The driver motioned for us to get in the back. We did and it started up the mud-filled road for town. About halfway there, the truck fish-tailed onto the shoulder and became stuck. We were not going very fast, so no one was hurt. Pero we did have to dig through the mud to get behind the truck to rock it loose. **(Takes a deep breath.)** Aye Dios. **(He seats himself.)**

We rocked and we pulled and pushed for what seemed like forever. Finally, in one quick move the truck shifted to the right, spinning the tires and whipping itself and Luisito into a tree, the truck crushed his chest. He died immediately. **(Serafín cradles his arms as if he were holding Luisito's body in them.)**

Luisito

Papá, did you try to save the world?

Serafín

No, hijo, no.

Scene 10

(Music up. Strains of a generic Italian opera are heard from offstage.)

Serafín

Rafaela Italiana, mi hermana, who lived on the ranchito with me and Lucio, was now singing Grand Opera in front of crowned heads and other gavachos. She sent us a postcard of a gran palacio in Europe. I threw it away. She also sent us money. I sent it back. If she was good enough to be a Mejicana when she was poor, why wasn't she a Mejicana now that she had money? Soon the war ended and we moved to Denver. All the young soldado razos returned. No longer young, no longer soldiers, pero still raza. They returned home after seeing the world and all its ugliness and here they saw signs that said, "No dogs or Mexicans Allowed!" Marialuisa found work at the May Company, a big department store in Denver. Once again she did bookkeeping. It was a good job, pero normalmente not one that they would give to a Mejicana. They thought she was Italian. She didn't deny it. I wonder how many Lozanos were going around eating spaghetti, just to keep their jobs. To this day, I hate spaghetti.

I woke up one morning to find myself alone en mi casa. All my hijos were grown and busy leading their own lives.

Scene 11

Serafin

Carlos, a donde vas?

Carlos

La casa de mi novia.

Serafin

Cual novia?

Carlos

Susana.

Serafin

I thought your novia was Leticia.

Carlos

Leti fue la semana pasada, ahora es Susana.

Serafín

Rosalia, para donde vas?

Rosalia

Out.

Serafin

Como que out?

Rosalia

Just out.

Serafín

Felipe, a donde vas?

Felipe

No se pero voy.

(Lucio Serafin's brother appears and sits, staring blankly at the wall)

Scene 12

Serafín

Bueno Lucio, parece que no mas queda nosotros. **(Not surprisingly Lucio doesn't answer)** Bueno pues, I guess you don't feel like talking. Is there something on that wall that you see, that I don't? You stare at it so. Maybe there's a window here and everything that ever happened is happening now, que no? Mira, there's Papa and the ranchito and Mama and the mission and there is you. Lucio, you're crying, you don't have to do that. You don't have to be scared. They can't hurt us no more, Lucio. Toma, I bought it this morning, es vino and it works.

29

Now tell me, when you were captured by the Japoneses, why did they make you walk to Bataan? **(Lucio drops the bottle.)** Pobrecito, mi hermano, they cut the tendons on his ankles, so he couldn't run away. Now, he can't run no more. Lucio?

Lucio

(Lucio rises to shuffle to the bathroom. He is very neat in his appearance and the slightest imperfection causes tremendous uneasiness.) Donde están las estijeras? Tengo un hilo suelto en mis pantalones y yo quiero cortarlo. **(He enters the bathroom.)**

Serafín

(Serafín waits at first patiently, but soon he begins to squirm. He walks to the bathroom door.) Apurate en el escusado, tengo que irme tambíen, andalé abre la puerta, Lucio. **(Serafín pushes his way into bathroom and disappears offstage. He re-enters.)** I broke open the door. I found the scissors and Lucio tambíen.

He used the scissors to cut himself off from the pain that haunted him. **(Pause.)** Once again I was alone.

Scene 13

(Serafín's children re-enter.)

Carlos

Buenos dias, Papa.

Serafín

Carlos, buenos dias.

Carlos

Papa, cuida mis niños, por favor.

Serafín

Y que paso con la mamá de ellos?

Carlos

Papa, its over between her and I. I want out.

Rosalia

Buenos dias, Papá.

Serafín

Rosalia.

Rosalia

Aqui están mis niños cuidalos, por favór.

Serafín

A donde vas?

Rosalia

Just out.

Felipe

Papá? Mis niños.

Serafín

Out! Out! Out! Todos quitense de mi.

(Blackout.)

Scene 14

Serafín

(Lights come up on Serafín who is crying and embracing Lucio's headstone. Today is the day of Lucio's funeral. He thinks he is alone. He is drinking from a bottle of wine.) Lucio, mi hermano, con un dedo Dios dio el hombre la vida, and with one finger he cuts the cord from this life and takes his last breath into the next.

It is afternoon and they have lowered your body into the ground, but your spirit roams and prowls the shadows, it shuffles each painful step in search of solace.

Rafaela

You are the big brother that guarded his life, now you guard his body after death.

Serafín

Rafaela, hermanita. (Realizing who she is.) Desgraciada.

Rafaela

When Lucio was a boy, I remember how he would always sleep with one leg out of the covers. You would come in at night and slip it back inside.

Serafín

He was afraid that if something happened, he would need to be able to move quickly.

Rafaela

Always moving, never stopping

Serafín

(Finishing her last line.) long enough to get caught. You have said your good-bye. Now, before you spoil your royal gown, leave.

Rafaela

Hermano, it is only you and I. This is the time we need each other most.

Serafín

Lucio and I once had a sister who was Mejicana. You have nothing I need.

Rafaela

So today you kill me as well.

Serafín

You have long been dead from my memory.

(Marialuisa enters.)

Marialuisa

No Fino. There has not been a day gone by when we should not thank Rafaela for the money she has sent us. Since you have been unable to work, what I earn has never been enough. Por favór Serafín, she is your sister.

Serafín

Toma tu dinero. **(He throws the change from his pocket. To Rafaela.)** Go act happy for the gringos, porque, we don't need you to act sad for us. **(He turns to Marialuisa.)** And you, all these years. you lied to me, you lied.

(He runs away from them and pauses, after reaching a safe distance, he drinks from the bottle of wine. He toasts Lucio and beats his hands to his chest. He throws himself to the ground and rests.)

Scene 15

Serafín

It is evening, and I look across the street at the house where I once lived.

I see the young girl who bore me four niños. They are moving her today. The wind whips cold across the trees. It is autumn. I see young men help a very tired old woman from the house. They call her abuela. She will go with them to California where it will always be warm. They will live there, together as a family. I watch, well hidden behind my liquor. They cannot see me, nor can they recognize me. I am an old drunkard. It has been years since I left the house. The old woman stops and smiles. She speaks. Marialuisa, mi amor, your smile is as warm as the day I married you.

Marialuisa

Esposo, I speak with the hope that one day this house will convey my pain, that of birth, that of life, that of the loneliness and helplessness of not being able to fight the demons that you were not strong enough to slay. Fino, this house knew love. Maybe you could not feel it, but I gave it. In these rooms there once was a man with whom I made love. I gave myself to you, and only you. Now there is a ghost that hides en botellas. Damn you! When you pass this house and see us gone, I want you to feel the pain and maybe someday you will feel the love. Adios mi esposo.

Serafín

(Reaches to touch Marialuisa, but he of course cannot. He begins to sob, reaches in his pocket for his hanky and a silver dollar falls from his pocket.) Where did this come from? (Serafín picks up the money and walks to a bar. He slams the dollar on the table. Music comes up from backstage. The song is a hard driving ranchera with accordion accompaniment.) Hombre, give me a glass of Tokay.

(He sips his drink slowly, to make it last. His hands tremble as he raises the glass to his lips. The bar door opens, letting the cold winter night into the warm glow of the Mexican Cantina.

Serafin turns to find Lucio standing next to him in the bar. Lucio is dressed in white linen pants and a white guayabera.) Que carajo! Lucio, que estás haciendo aqui? You can walk and you're not dead. Wait a minute, am I dead?

Lucio

Todavia no, pero mira. **(Lucio shows Serafín that his body is in fact lying between two buildings.)** It is much warmer in here, better music and maybe even a little pierna. Mira, if you want help, just say so. If you just lean up against the door it will open, someone will help you.

Serafín

What makes you think I want help? What makes you think I want anything from anybody?

Lucio

Orgulloso hasta el fin, y te digo que ya será el fin. Besides there are better ways to kill yourself. Ask me, I know. By the way have you seen the scissors? I have a string coming loose on my pants. **(To bartender who is not seen.)** Oiga señor, dos mas por favor. **(To Serafín.)** Besides, after you kill yourself you just end up dead. Ask me, I know.

Serafín

Lucio, I saw Papá.

Lucio

You are loco.

Serafín

Lucio, I talked to him too.

Lucio

(Again to bartender.) Señor, two doubles. Fino, Papá is dead.

Serafin

So are you.

Lucio

Okay. So what did he say?

Serafín

He said to get up.

Lucio

Hay 'sta. He wants to save you, tambíen.

Serafín

No, he said to get up and go to work on the ranchito. And you know, I saw Mama and Don Pelón and Sebastían. And Luisito was alive. Lucio, all my life I have fought to survive in Los United Estates. I gave everything I had to give a long time ago. They can take no more from me. I will not allow them to make me live. Hermano, I choose to die.

Lucio

Bueno, if that is your choice, I am here to guide you. It is time. **(The music stops abruptly, they move out to the alley. Serafín lies down, in the snow. One of the punks has returned. Lucio watches from the shadows.)**

Punk #1

Hey old man, get up. I decided that I don't want you to die. You ain't worth shit and I won't have you on my conscience. Did you hear me? Godammit get up. Answer me. I said answer me.

Serafín

(Serafin looks the punk squarely in the eye.) Fuck you!

(The punk becomes very angry and begins to hit Serafín.
Serafín grabs the punk and begins to choke strangle him. After
all the years of working with his hands he has one last act of
strength.

As the life drains out of the punk, Serafín releases him. Both
the punk and Serafin struggle to regain their faculties. The
punk gets up. Before leaving he gives Serafín one last kick in
the stomach. Serafín curls up. The punk exits. Serafín leans
back against the wall and dies. Lucio covers Serafín's body with
old newspapers. One leg slips out from under the newspaper
covering. Lucio tucks it back under the newspaper. Marialuisa
appears on stage and places Serafín's hat in her hands together
with Lucio. As if posing for a Sears portrait, they form a final
tableau.)

El fin

Little Hands Hold the Wind

Little Hands Hold the Wind
written and directed by Anthony J. García
Produced by Millie Durán

Cast of Characters

El Viento- an all knowing female entity whose age is eternal.
Amalia-7 years old little girl.
Ana-Amalia's mother.
Marialuisa-15 year girl celebrating her quinceañera.
Vitorio- 19 year old son of Estrella Moreno.
Estrella Moreno-Beautiful curandera y bruja.
Felipito-Son of Don Felipe and Marialuisa's brother
Don Felipe Flores-Rich and powerful, dueño of the Flores Ranchito.
Señora Flores- Wife of Don Felipe, mother of Marialuisa and Felipito.
Big Jim Daniels-Powerful rancher and businessman, friend of Don Felipe.
Tio Lupe-Gentleman in his late '60's he is a storyteller.
Padre Seco-Pampered pastor of la Iglesia de Nuestra Señora de los Pobres Siempres.
Don Domingo-Street performer in the "Carpa" tradition his traveling tent shows inform and entertain the, " gente " of the brush country.

Little Hands Hold the Wind

Little Hands Hold the Wind was commissioned as a one-woman play by Ruby Nelda Perez, a tremendously talented female actor from San Antonio, Texas. Ruby along with her husband Jorge Piña, and their daughter Alma became a second family for me, during my residency at the Guadalupe Cultural Arts Center. Jorge is the director of the Theater Arts Program at the GCAC. This play is based on Ruby's impressions of growing up in South Texas.

The play has had readings at the Colorado Dance Festival, in Boulder, Colorado, in which Ruby performed. *Little Hands Hold the Wind* was presented by Ernesto Ravetto for Theater Adelante/Teatro Nuestro at the 2nd Annual Festival Latino of New Play readings, which is produced by El Teatro de la Esperanza, Teatro Mission, Latin American Theater Artists, Theater Adelante/Teatro Nuestro and the Latino Theater Lab.

The cast for the reading was as follows:

Saturday July 30, 1994

El Viento	Rosa María Escalante
Tia Lupe	Wilma Bonét
Ana/Estrella Moreno	Dena Martinez
Amalia	Mikiko Thelwell
Don Felipe	Michael Torres
Padre Seco/Señor Daniels	Richard Ruyle
Marialuisa	Greta Sanchez-Ramirez
Felipito	Davíd Acevedo
Narrator/Señora Flores	Tessa Koening-Martinez

Little Hands Hold the Wind

(El Viento enters, she is dressed in a flowing dress. Bells, chimes and fluttering curtains accompany her entrance.)

El Viento

I floated in on a hot afternoon in the South Texas town of Alma. I whipped the dirt up on the dry, thirsty streets. I found an open window in the Church of Nuestra Señora de los Almas Perdidos, the candles all bowed to me as I passed, much the same way the trees bend their branches to acknowledge my presence. As I brushed up against the confessional curtains, I saw tiny fingers connected to fervent palms, the fingers entwined in holy beads. Now before I go any further, I need to tell you that all Texas towns have hot afternoons, but not all of them are called Alma, and not all of them have little hands that can hold the wind. As I moved closer, I heard her words,

Amalia

(Praying to a statue of San Antonio.) I don't know if you are really up there? **(To herself.)** But when I am in here all alone, I sometimes feel that you are real, that you follow me with your eyes. **(She crosses maintaining eye contact with the statue.)** Once I knocked over the Holy Water bowl. I picked it up and when I looked over my shoulder, I was sure that I saw you frowning. Then, when I filled a cup full of water from the horse trough and poured it in with the Holy Water left in the bowl, I saw you frown and I was so afraid that you would step down from your spot and spank me. **(To San Antonio.)** But you didn't and now here I am asking you for a favor. Pero you are San Antonio and you find lost things. And what I want you to find for me is something pretty important. It's pretty big too. I don't know that you can do it, and if you can't, well just tell me, because I understand that you can do some things and some things you can't. San Antonio, por favor, I want you to find my Papi. I didn't lose him, pero I don't have him and I want him.

El Viento

Kind of breaks your heart don't it? **(Breathing a sigh of relief.)** Whew. **(Holding back emotion.)** You know, I'm supposed to be above this sort of thing. **(Trying to laugh.)** Get it?

You know the wind, high above. Ahh... forget it. **(Taking out a set of bells, she rings it. She listens.)** I love it when I do that.

(She does it again, for effect. Rumbling of drums. El Viento begins to move furiously about the stage.) Racing through the town, the night is halfway between sunlight and darkness, a blue-gray sky covers Alma, the pueblito is calm now.

As I pass a rusty shack, that someone calls home, I stop. Someone has been kind enough to place these on their front porch.

(She indicates the bells and rings them once again. A high pitched whistling sound interrupts.) "Who is that?" the niño asks, "It is just the wind" la Mama contesta. **(Indignant.)** Just the wind. When I push the cool clouds in to shield the sun, no one says it is, "just the wind". If it is just the wind, why doesn't everyone do it. **(To audience)** Come on you try it. Come on blow. **(Puffs cheeks, making it appear difficult)** Some of those clouds are like heifers, you ever try to get a cow to move out of the shade a couple of hundred miles?. **(with pride)** But I can do it. **(Bumps her hips and snaps her fingers.)** Like that. **(Rings bells again.)** Everyone likes to hear the sound of their own voice.

It is night time and the child cannot sleep. She hears me whistling through the cracks in the broken down wooden shanty. It sounds like a child's gentle crying, "I'm frightened" says the child. "It is just the wind." says the Mama. No mija it is not, "just" the wind, it is the mighty wind. The powerful wind, the Hurucán of the ancient days that created the swirl of energy that gave birth to the universe. It is I who has come to hum a lonely lullaby, so rest warmly tonight as the wind will blow all evil away from you. **(Pause.)** But as I pass through the streets, the Saturday night tension vibrates from the cantinas, from the ranchitos where the week-long, hard work with little pay life, begins to boil over.

(Music up, traditional conjunto instruments are heard. Marialuisa and Rafael dance alone on-stage.)

On the Flores Ranchito, they have slaughtered a steer. It is Marialuisa's quinceañera. Don Felipe Flores is her father. He is a businessman, whose family has always had money. While the men and women of Alma scratch out a hand-to-mouth existence, Don Felipe and his family have prospered here in the valle. Many people say it is because he is a favorite of Señor Daniels. Some say it is because his grandfather made a deal with the devil. I say it is because the Flores and Daniels family made a deal to split the wealth in the brush country, and make sure that no one else got anything. Everyone is related here, and if your cousin did something to my cousin then we are enemies.

Tonight, Marialuisa is fifteen, she is a woman. Her father has presented her to the family and townspeople. Rafael Hernandez is her escort, he is also Felipito's best friend.

(Felipito appears on stage. He smiles approvingly at Marialuisa and Rafael.)

Felipito is her older brother.

(Don Felipe and Señora Flores enter and cross to Felipito. They are pleased with the evening.)

Don Felipe likes Rafael, la Señora Flores likes Rafael.

(Marialuisa and Rafael have stopped dancing.)

Naturally, Marialuisa thinks Rafael is...

Marialuisa

Okay. **(Marialuisa begins to dance with her father.)**

El Viento

As she dances her vals, her gaze drifts across the crowd until two midnight dark eyes steal her. **(The dance music continues and everyone drifts away except Marialuisa and Vitorio.)** The brush provides cover, as the coyotes serenade to the moon. Vitorio, the bruja's son waits. His eyes are wild, and in the milk white light of the mother moon, they flash like the black rock the ancients carved into weapons. It was called obsidian. In the reflection of Vitorio's black eyes, Marialuisa danced. Her white quinceañera dress, becoming a moon unto itself, caught up in the moment, I ran my fingers through her hair and brushed it outward. **(Laughing.)**

Hijole, pobre muchacho never had a chance. Que onda, eh raza?

Marialuisa

(She moves to Vitorio.) You were watching me. I felt your eyes while I danced. It was as though everyone disappeared. When I looked again and you were gone. Aren't you afraid?

Vitorio

Aren't you?

El Viento

Marialuisa looked up to get lost in that deep pool of eyes. And as Vitorio touched her hand, the searing heat raced through her heart.

Marialuisa

My Papa knows I like you. He has warned me about you. He says your Mama is a witch and that she wants to harm me.

Vitorio

My Mama is a witch, and I am her son. But neither of us has ever committed an act of evil. We do not steal from the poor, like Señor Daniels, we do not kill rancheros in back alleys. (Vitorio is angry and for the first time Marialuisa is afraid.)

Marialuisa

Stop it. I don't want to hear you talk about my Papa like that.

El Viento

As I moved past them, the tail-end of a gust brought the words of a muffled scream and a cry for help. Marialuisa did not hear Vitorio, say, "I'm sorry". They both turned and ran through the moonlit brush, scattering jackrabbits in their path. Vitorio arrived first. Felipito, Don Felipe's only hijo, turned. His face lit with madness, his eyes flaming red, the scratches on his face burned a streak of blood down his face.

His shirt was ripped and he spoke in a voice that Vitorio had heard only in the incantations of the evil ones, the spirits of death and hatred.

Felipito

No woman refuses the son of Felipe Flores. It is not that I find you so irresistible, it is only that you refuse me and you must be taught a lesson. You, a campesino's daughter, should be honored that I would want to take you.

Mercedes

Por favór Felipito, let me go. **(Felipito pulls her to her knees. She tries to move but his hand is twisted into her hair. He raises his fist to strike her again. Vitorio emerges from the brush.)**

Felipito

(Startled) You? What do you want here? This is none of your affair. **(He hesitates but can't escape Vitorio's glare.)**

I warn you Vitorio, hijo de la bruja mala, you cannot intimidate me with your evil eyes. My father and I are too worldly to be victims of foolish superstitions. Your devil-worshipping mother may frighten old women and ignorant townspeople, but I do not hold such sentiments. Now, leave me alone or I will use this hunting knife to gut you like a common pig. Your life means as much to me as hers.

El Viento

Marialuisa stepped forward from the protecting brush. Her face was horror struck at the sight of the beaten young woman and her brother, a glistening knife blade in his hand.

Felipito

(Realizing that Marialuisa has been with Vitorio, he is now even more furious.) Is this the woman that danced with my father this evening? What was it he was offering to the world with such pride? Marialuisa, you are not a woman. You are just a foolish child.

45

Go back to the fiesta. Vitorio, Witch-boy, you have been warned to stay away from my Papa's rancho. This time you must be taught a lesson.

El Viento

Marialuisa turned to leave, it was a natural reaction. She had always done what her father and older brother had commanded. She hesitated only because she knew that this time, if she denied Vitorio, the chance existed that she would not see him again. She turned to tell her brother no, that she would see whomever she wanted. She was a woman, she was now fifteen. Wasn't that what a quinceañera was all about? I don't know what it is about human beings, why they seek to harm beyond reparation.

As I rushed and paced through the trees, pushing and shoving, attempting to change a force in the fates, Felipito, crazed by the moon, drunk with the scent of blood, brought the hunting knife down and plunged into the heart of the poor peasant child. Hopeless and faceless, her spirit left her on a lonely night in the South Texas moonlight. Vitorio, attempted to place himself between the blade and the girl. He was too late, as the three bodies tumbled to the ground. The lifeless child between the angry men, they rolled down the hill to the arroyo, until only two rolled and then only one moved. Emerging from the creek, his white shirt stained with the once warm blood of two souls, and turning a tear sparked its' reflection on his cheek, it was Vitorio.

Marialuisa

(Realizing her brother is dead, shouts angrily.) I hate you.

(Lights down. In black there is the sound of a terrible gale, crashing and general turmoil.)

El Viento

That night, an angry wind ruled Alma as the clapboard window coverings swung open and closed, creating a banging that allowed no soul to rest. The streets became a blizzard of dust and debris. On opposite sides of town two mothers called for their children.

(In shadow, Mercedes' mother and Señora Flores appear. They

46

are calling for their children, as if asking them to come in from playing. Their voices are not heard instead, a lamenting wailing is made by the wind.)

Señora Flores

Mijo donde estás?

Mercedes' Mother

Mija donde estás?

El Viento

I carried their voices to the moon blackening clouds. The clouds would rain, carrying their pleas back to earth. Murdered souls cannot reply, they can but echo.

(Felipito and Mercedes appear holding candles in their hands and move directly toward their mothers, who cannot see them and gesture as if to call them. Felipito and Mercedes only echo.)

Felipito

Me mataron.

Mercedes

Me mataron.

(El Viento blows and the candles go out.)

El Viento

It was at this point that I wondered why I did not leave Alma. But I stayed. And if the truth be known, this was not the first time an injustice had been committed in the name of passion. As the sun climbed over the eastern horizon, the impatient cock rousted his hens from slumber. The Sunday morning church bells called the town to assembly. Today they rang with a sense of urgency, porque el pueblo esta de luto. I carried their sound out to the farthest ranchitos and pueblitos.

This was Alma's pain and the entire county would know.

(Several townspeople enter, they are a buzz.)

They filed into the little church por la Misa de los Pobres Siempres. The word had carried through the town that the rinches, the Texas Rangers as the gringos called them, were hunting after Vitorio.

(Estrella Moreno enters.)

When his mother, Estrella Moreno, arrived in church the parishioners whispered.

(Don Felipe and Señora Flores enter.)

Don Felipe arrived in his expensive carriage with his wife, Señora Flores. Watching with big eyes and absorbing every minute of the action was Amalia. Usually she hated getting up, putting on a clean white dress and wasting a good morning's sleep, just to hear Padre Seco go on about sin, salvation and collection plate donations. Amalia turned from her front row pew and saw a big white man enter.

Amalia

Mamá?

El Viento

Her mother shushed her.

(Amalia's Mamá, Ana is sitting with Amalia.)

Ana

Shh.

Amalia

Pero Mama...

48

El Viento

Amalia could not contain herself. This time, her mother gave her a glare that indicated a spanking would follow the next outburst. Her fully widened eyes would soon be accompanied by a gaping mouth. The figure of Big Jim Daniels sat across the aisle, next to the sullen Don Felipe Flores.

Señor Daniels

Now, I don't want you to worry Felipe. We are going to catch this witch's son. The Rangers are tracking him right now. Before the week is out, I will bring your son's murderer to you, alive or dead.

(Don Felipe raises his bowed head, his eyes are red and pained. He looks at Señor Daniels for hope.)

This I promise you my friend.

(Señor Daniels grips Don Felipe's arm tightly to reinforce his promise.)

A town cannot be ruled by lawlessness. It is for the lawmakers to also enforce their laws. Alma will know justice.

El Viento

Padre Seco began to speak and the churchgoers settled into their most comfortable positions for the long morning.

(Padre Seco is a bumbling type, with matted white hair. It is usually combed and neatly parted in the middle, however this morning due to the tumultuous circumstances of the previous evening, it was pointed in every direction as if trying to escape his head.)

The altar boys slept, the choir yawned. Padre Seco, his ancient bones used to the comfort of a warm bed, hot coffee and a full breakfast, mumbled through his sermon.

Padre Seco

Our God is a vengeful God. He is kind to those who serve him. He rewards them and keeps them close to his mother's bosom.

(At the mention of the word bosom two boys giggle. Their mother's glance quells their excitement. Padre Seco continues.) But for those who practice evil, those who lurk about in the shadows of darkness, there is only one fate. Damnation. The Lord will have his vengeance.

El Viento

At that moment all eyes turned to Estrella Moreno. She held her head erect. Padre Seco, now backed by the congregation, boldly increased his assault on the unseen evil.

Padre Seco

It is God who will have his revenge on those who challenge his rule. You will be banished, banished from his sight, and for eternity you will burn.

El Viento

The reverent prayed, the curious stared and the, "holier than thou," cursed. Estrella Moreno. The witch stood. Everyone gasped.

(Padre Seco faints dead to the ground. Before a hushed crowd, Estrella Moreno moves to Don Felipe who will not look at her. Big Jim stands and places his hand on his pistol.)

Estrella Moreno

Señora Flores, last night we both lost our sons. In pain, we bore them and now in pain, we lose them. I am sorry for your pain. May Felipito rest in peace. I will light a candle to guide his journey. Marialuisa, mija, beg my son to stay away. You must never see him again. It was not meant for you and him to be together. If he comes to you, they will kill him. When he sends word to you, tell him to go.

El Viento

At this moment a tear escaped Estrella Moreno's eye. It fell along her brown cheekbones and landed on Marialuisa's hand. And it burned, yet it toothed. Unconsciously, she touched it to her cheek where it mixed with her rapidly falling tears and once again the burning soothed. Amalia was sure that she was witnessing the most spectacular of events.

Her eyes darted from the stunned parishioners, the fainted Padre Seco, the armed Big Jim Daniel's and the three mourning women. She could not absorb the action fast enough.

Amalia

Mamá, if church is like this every Sunday, let's come early and get better seats.

El Viento

Estrella Moreno left the church having said her piece. Señor Daniels and the Flores family left together, as the altar boys hovered over the fainted body of Padre Seco. When the Ladies of Holy Sodality of la Virgen Chismosa rose, they did so in unison. Their cackling voices sounded similar to that of the hens being brought to the church for Padre Seco's blessing.

(Amalia and her mother Ana rise to leave.)

Amalia

Mamá, if Padre Seco's blessings make everything better, why doesn't he just bless himself so he doesn't faint?

El Viento

Away from the crowded Sunday afternoon church plaza, far down the flat road that leads into town, a large smiling soul paused.

(Tio Lupe enters.)

He looked ahead at the town, sensed the anguish, and debated whether to continue or to take his stories on to the next town. That night, Tio Lupe knocked on the wooden door at Amalia's house.

Amalia

Mamá there is someone at the door. **(She looks toward the door and awaits an answer.)** Okay I'll get it. **(She opens the door and looks up at the imposing figure leaning inward.)** Mamá, it's a giant. **(Amalia calls to her mother again.)** Mamá, are you expecting a giant?

Tio Lupe

Ana, you don't remember me? Soy yo, el Tio Lupe.

Amalia

I don't know any Tio Lupe.

Tio Lupe

I don't understand. The last time I came to Alma there was a little girl, tiny and pretty just like you. Her name was Ana.

Amalia

Mamá is named Ana.

Tio Lupe

(Tio Lupe is shocked.) It can't be. It was only a short time ago that I came through here telling stories. There was a little girl who had a head full of dreams. I gave her stories and she gave me hot chocolaté. She was only 6 years old.

El Viento

Pobre Lupe never understood that time must pass for everyone, except him.

Lupe and I had been friends for a very long time, since he was a boy working the citrus crop in the Valley. I was responsible for the creases in his face. The sun had made his skin leathery, but I placed the character lines around his eyes. Lupe always had special hands, hands that were strong but gentle to the touch, big hands that could caress a tiny orange, unsheathing it's coarse covering and never damaging the delicate underskin, which he would also peel, leaving only the sweetest most tender portion. It was his hands that you noticed, a boy with a man's hands. Large and firm when he greeted you, but graceful when he gestured to tell you a story.

Tio Lupe

So many people live their lives only aware of how difficult life is. Others know immediately the forces that exist around you. Niños, you must know that dreams are more powerful than worries. While many curse their lives, you must use your life to paint pictures. I use words.

El Viento

It seems that he was always like this. I remember him, a seven-year-old chavalón, working out in the grove, hearing me rustle the leaves. Before I could hide, he shouted.

Tio Lupe

(As a boy.) "Mama, did you see her? Es el viento."

El Viento

From then on it was fun and games-hide and seek, tag. Often, we would walk together along the Rio Grande and we would talk. Lupe had a gift and one wish that he could receive only as a man.

Now an elderly gentleman, with his long white hair tied behind his head, he appeared at Amalia's door.

Tio Lupe

I'm sorry mija, I must have the wrong house.

(Before Amalia can answer, El Viento pushes the door open. She pushes so hard that she loses her balance and tumbles into the casita. It is in this moment that she lets her guard down and a stunned Amalia sees her. Amalia gasps, then covers her eyes and peaks out, looking between them. Lupe smiles to see El Viento spread out on the floor. He looks quickly at Amalia, who just as quickly covers her eyes again.)

Do you see her?

(Amalia shakes her stunned head yes. She covers her eyes once again.)

Don't hide your eyes. Look quickly, because she will be gone just as quickly.

(Amalia once again looks between her fingers.)

Come let us help her up. Now step back and watch out for her tail wind.

(El Viento hurriedly gathers herself. She exits through a window and the doors slam shut. Mamá calls out from offstage.)

Ana

Amalia, what was all that noise?

Amalia

Nothing Mamá, just the wind.

(Amalia and Tio Lupe snicker.)

El Viento

It serves me right.

Ana

Amalia, you better not make a mess in the house. (As Ana approaches the doorway, her eyes open wide. She is once again the little

Ana that Tio Lupe had come to visit 20 years ago. She cries out)
Tio Lupe.

(She jumps into his arms and embraces him.) You promised you
would come back. I waited for you. Will you please stay for supper?
**(Realizing that she is now grown, and that Tio Lupe has already
met Amalia, she introduces them.)** Tio Lupe, this is Amalia, she is
my daughter. Say hi to Tio Lupe.

(Amalia manages a weak begrudging acknowledgment.)

Amalia

Buenas noches, Tio Lupe.

Ana

Please Tio Lupe, come in. Mija, please set the table so Tio Lupe can
join us. I'm sorry it's not much, some frijolitos, helote, and some pan de
campo. I wish it were more.

Tio Lupe

Ana, you offer a feast. It is a fine Sunday dinner and I am grateful for
the invitation.

**(Tio Lupe washes his hands and sits at the table to eat. Amalia
sits next to him. They exchange glances. She starts to fold her
hands to pray but stops and looks up at Tio Lupe. Amalia
whispers.)**

Amalia

Are you really our Tio?

(Tio Lupe frowns.)

Okay, but if you aren't, then you shouldn't eat as much. **(Pause.)** It's
just that you look like you could eat a lot, and Mamá also made arroz de
leche and ...

(Amalia looks up, noticing that her Mamá is watching her, she returns to prayer.) Dear God, please bless our food. Remember how you made a little bit of bread and fishes go a long way so that everybody got to eat something sweet afterwards? Well, that's kind of the way things are here. We only have a little bit of food, and an extra person, who looks like they eat a lot, is here for supper. I know it was a long time ago when you did that miracle, but do you think you can try real hard to remember it?

(She feels her mother's eyes on her, and changes the subject.) Also God, if San Antonio comes by and asks you about a favor, and it sounds like a pretty big one, well that's mine. Do you think that you can help him out? **(She looks up once again and then finishes.)** Thank you and your son for giving us food, even though there might not be enough, because now we have someone extra joining us for dinner. Amen.

El Viento

Amalia finished her meal quietly, watching all the time each serving that Tio Lupe served himself. It seemed as though he would never finish, but he did. When the sweet tasting canela flavored rice was set on the table, Amalia, Tio Lupe and Mamá ate their fill. Amalia said one last silent prayer of thanks. It was now time for the special surprise. The moment Mama had waited for, as Tio Lupe moved his chair closer to the burning fireplace. He rolled a cigarette, lit it, and drawing a deep breath of smoke, he exhaled. A cloud filled the room. Amalia scrunched her face to let everyone know that she objected to the smell. Mamá sat on the floor, beckoning Amalia, to curl up on her lap. Tio Lupe cleared his voice, his large body and long hair silhouetted by the burning fireplace, began to speak. I found myself straining to hear. I crept closer, inching down the fireplace, at one point, causing the embers to spark and dance out on the dirt floor.

Tio Lupe noticed and smiled. He began his story by cutting the air with his strong magical hands.

Tio Lupe

Three months ago, it seems like. I was walking down the dirt roads. I was further north, but not as far as San Antonio, because I never go into the city. Cities eat you alive with all the noise and people rushing. No one hears the other voices that speak. No one hears the bird's warning, the coyotes joking or the jackrabbits complaining.

This day the clouds were mooing like fat Mama cows, because the wind was moving them South and you could hear the wind huffing and puffing, taking every bit of energy to move them to a place where they might be more needed.

It was hot, and I was glad that the clouds were being moved in my direction. I heard a gentle note, carried in a tin cup to my ears by the wind.

Then I heard a clash of cymbals that was not made by thunder. I saw a reflection of sunlight bouncing brilliantly in the distance. I naturally moved in the direction of the noise, as curious as the people who arrived before me and less anxious than those who arrived after me. A man introduced himself to those of us who had gathered around him.

Don Domingo

(**While clanging a cymbal.**) Señoras y Señores, muy buena gente, bienvenidos al Teatro Domingo, presented to you by la familia Domingo. And who am I? I am Domingo, of course. My good friends, every week my family and I travel to a different town to tell the stories that have long been a part of our lives. The stories told by the ancient ones, as well as stories told by compadres to compadres and comadres to comadres. Teatro Domingo brings you all the latest chisme, please remember you heard it here first. All we ask, is that if you like the play, if it made you laugh, if it made you cry. and heaven forbid, if it made you think, that you express your gratitude by placing a coin, several coins, several large coins into my sombrero, which I will happily offer at the appropriate time. (**Don Domingo pulls a curtain across stage and begins the production.**) Many people say that Texas is the largest place in the entire world. Many people believe that the state was built by great men, with great dreams and lots of Mejicanos to work for them. This is the story of one such man. A man who believed his own legend.

Tio Lupe

And the play began. A child appeared on stage, she knelt before a shrine of an invisible goddess. She closed her eyes and the tears escaped. Although her clothes were meager, she held her head high. She prayed, not for clothes, nor did she ask for food. The town, you see, was being controlled by a terrible evil. She knew that there was a time when the Mexican rancheros herded their cattle. No one man was more powerful than another. Until one day, a stranger arrived from the east. He fenced off large tracts of land.

He turned neighbor against neighbor. Soon, water that had been shared by all, belonged to only one man. Judges, sheriffs and the Texas Rangers also belonged to the stranger.

Slowly, the sky darkened and a shadowy figure appeared on stage. It began to approach the kneeling child. In the moment that he would have grabbed her, her Papa, from nowhere stepped forward and began to battle the figure. The more the Papa struggled, the larger the shadowy figure grew. Until, in one large flash, accompanied by lightening and thunder they both disappeared.

Amalia

The Papi disappeared?

Tio Lupe

Si mija.

Amalia

That's sad.

Tio Lupe

No mija, it seems that the Papa had been calling on the townsfolk to rise up against the stranger. Now, it was for the daughter to keep faith and help defeat the stranger. It was not easy. The young child had never known her father well, as this event had happened a long time ago. She told herself, on nights when she lay awake crying, that she did not miss him, but she did. She remembered her dream, to be free of the shadowy stranger.

One more time the shadowy figure appeared. This time, the young child was ready for it. As she knelt, she pretended not to notice the figure approaching. As it moved, so close that she could smell its' horrible breath, she quickly slipped beneath his grasp, moving behind it. She realized that it was the stranger holding the wires, and when she cut them, the ghostly figure dropped harmlessly to the ground. The audience, realizing that this meant the defeat of the stranger, cheered. Don Domingo, who had been playing the part of the stranger, removed his mask and stepped forward to speak to the audience.

Don Domingo

We all know the evil that controls our lives. What are we to do? What will we do?

Tio Lupe

With that, he passed his sombrero through the crowd and collected the money.

Amalia

What happened to the Papi? Was he dead?

Tio Lupe

No mija, her Papi was not dead. The stranger had placed him in jail.

El Viento

With a sigh, Tio Lupe looked at Ana.

Tio Lupe

He is not dead.

El Viento

He looked at Amalia.

Tio Lupe

I must go. Amalia, will you sleep well tonight, for me?

Amalia

Si, Tio Lupe. **(Amalia embraces Lupe, kisses her Mamá and crawls off to bed.)**

El Viento

With these words, Tio Lupe disappeared into the rapidly falling night. Lupe was a good soul. He had delivered his message of hope and I was pleased that he had answered my call. You see, when Lupe grew to manhood, he found himself in South Texas. He was a husband and a father, stretching out a small life with an even smaller ranchito. His land, however, was in Big Jim Daniel's way. One night, he returned to find his place burned to the ground. His family was gone. They had been scared away, far away. In his anguish, Lupe called to me. His boyhood wish had been to share his gift of storytelling. He asked me to remove his pain, and in return, he would give his stories to the children of the brush country. I accepted his promesa.

Saturday roared in, like a feverish Texas dust devil, with people moving briskly through the town. Not far from the town, amid secluded covering, Estrella Moreno lived. True to her name, she was darkly beautiful, her black hair was silver-streaked and her oval-shaped eyes radiated the deep passion in her heart. Now, in the dying daylight, she began to light candles before her humble altar. She touched the incense with fire, the billowing smoke filled the room with the wisdom of the copal. She looked through the clouds into the mirror, looking for some sign to allow her to glimpse what was to be. As she prayed, she looked deeply into her reflection to see a second pair of Indio eyes. She turned quickly, the image remained.

Estrella Moreno

Mijo, you take a terrible risk coming here, pero I knew you would. I was afraid that I could not protect you. So I did this...**(She indicates the candles and smiles.)** I suppose you bring out the bruja in me. Give your Mama un abrazo.

(Vitorio emerges from the shadows, and the mother and son embrace. She composes herself.)

Ándale mijo, sit I made caldo for you.

(Vitorio eats as if he is starving and has not eaten in days.)

Slow down mijo. Don't try to eat it all at once. You know that every rinche in this half of the state is looking for you, and if any of Señor Daniels' or Don Felipe's men find you first, pues they will kill you on the spot.

What's that? Quiet?

El Viento

A lechusa flew to the tree outside the window. Her voice was deep and warning. Vitorio instinctively hid. The bruja, hiding a kitchen knife in her skirt, approached the window.

Estrella Moreno

You can stop hiding. I know you are out there. Show yourself.

(From the shadows, Marialuisa emerges. She steps, timidly, into the light.)

Come in quickly, everyone has probably followed you.

El Viento

Vitorio, seeing Marialuisa, moved to let the candles illuminate his face. Estrella Moreno gestures for them to sit. Amid the flickering candles and the rising moon, the sound of the hoof beats grew.

Estrella Moreno

Niños, there are many things in this world that you two do not understand. Tonight you will witness the truth in all it's ugliness. I have seen it and it will come to pass. Please sit, there is no need to hurry. Marialuisa your father approaches.

(Vitorio sits and finishes his caldo. Estrella Moreno pours chocolaté for the girl, cuts pieces of pan de campo and places her knife alongside the steaming cup on the table.)

El Viento

Within minutes the riders had arrived. Don Felipe approached the doorway to Estrella Moreno's house.

Don Felipe

Estrella Moreno, we have many riders. You must send Vitorio out. Justice demands that he be punished.

(The door opens and Marialuisa steps into the doorway. Don Felipe calls to his men.)

Hold you fire! That is Marialuisa. Hold your fire! Es mi hija. Estrella Moreno, now you are holding my daughter. Release her immediately. I demand in the name of righteousness.

Marialuisa

No Papa, I am staying. **(Pausing briefly.)** I know Papa. Everything. know.

El Viento

Now the night was filled with silence, barely interrupted by the sound of the lechusas calling and the horses exhaling in the humid air. Don Felipe signaled his men, then dismounted and approached the house. He looked at Big Jim Daniels who clearly disapproved.

Marialuisa

Papa is coming in.

Estrella Moreno

Está bien.

El Viento

When Don Felipe entered the small doorway his face was hardly that of the dashing horseman of his youth, who dazzled the women at the charreadas. Seeing Vitorio holding his faded and worn pistola, Don Felipe stopped.

Estrella Moreno

Mijo, place the pistola on the mesa. Felipe, you may feel safe, I bear you no harm.

El Viento

Don Felipe looked at Vitorio, for the first time, directly in the eyes.

Don Felipe

You have your mother's eyes. As a child I watched you. Always, you were a constant reminder of your mother, and I wanted you to go away. When my son was born, he was to be everything to me, the one to carry on. But you were always there. A reminder of a world I left far behind me. Do you hate me? I am your father, do you hate me?

(Vitorio does not answer.)

You killed my son, and now more than ever I hate you. **(The room is silent. Don Felipe turns to Marialuisa.)** Have you made love to him?

Marialuisa

(Shocked.) Papa no.

Estrella Moreno

Felipe, after all these years, our road leads us here. When I first saw you, you were the most dashing man that ever rode the brush in South Texas. Hijos, did you know that your Papa was a singer of romantic ballads?

(Don Felipe is not enjoying this.)

What lovely words you would sing. Your Papa was such an honorable man, when he found out I was going to have his baby, he offered to take me to a doctor to, "correct the problem." You see Marialuisa, your grandfather had an important name, but he did not have the money to do business with Señor Daniels. Your mother's family did though. A pregnant Indita would ruin your grandfather's plan. When I refused your grandfather's help, the two of them made sure everyone in town thought that I was not only evil, but a tramp.

Don Felipe

I don't have to answer to you, witch. Your soul will burn in hell.

Estrella Moreno

Don Felipe Flores, this witch would not trade souls with you.

Marialuisa

Papa, Felipito killed the girl. Vitorio tried to save her. I saw it, Papa.

(Señor Daniels' voice interrupts.)

Señor Daniels

Don Felipe I am tired of waiting. Let us end the foolishness. I am coming in.

(Vitorio glares angrily at Don Felipe.)

Don Felipe

Señor Daniels you must enter unarmed.

Señor Daniels

(Jim Daniels enters in a brusque manner. To Vitorio.) You are a murderer son, and you are going to die.

Marialuisa

He is not. I saw that he was trying to help.

(Señor Daniels, realizing that Marialuisa knows enough to pose a danger, looks at Don Felipe as if to say, "Are you going to take care of this?)

Don Felipe

It doesn't matter, mija. There is more here at stake. He must die.

Marialuisa

Vitorio is not the murderer here, Señor Daniels, am I right? Vitorio is not the first man who will die for your greed. The man who saw you kill is no more. If I am a witness, will you remove me also?

Señor Daniels

(Señor Daniels moving to the door.)

The house will be burnt to the ground. The witch and her son will die. Don Felipe will you order your men?

Marialuisa

Papa will you kill me too?

Don Felipe

(Don Felipe rises, a sad and beaten man.) Marialuisa, you must never tell anyone what has taken place tonight. It would be very bad.

Marialuisa

Would it be worse than killing people to take their land? Would it be worse than buying judges and sheriffs? Worse than turning the rinches loose on your own people? Worse than living a lie? Papa, I will not leave this house.

Don Felipe

(Don Felipe's face hardens. Looking Marialuisa in the eye he speaks to Señor Daniels.) I will give the men the order.

El Viento

At this point Don Felipe's heart was as black as the burning eyes that peered at him. They moved to leave, opening the small casita door only to find Señora Flores waiting.

(The men stand immobilized and watch as Señora Flores steps between them. She crosses to Estrella Moreno.)

Señora Flores

For years I hated you. You were everything I was not, mysterious, romantic and beautiful. I always knew that my husband was in love you. At nights after we would make love, he would walk to the window and stare at the swirling clouds passing the moon. I heard the lechusa's call and I always felt he was looking for you, wanting you. **(To Don Felipe.)** When my father first brought you to the house to meet his plain daughter, my heart flew. I was sixteen and you were the most handsome man in the brush country.

I loved you when you told me of your dreams to build a rancho that would breed the finest cattle, cattle which would feed everyone, rich and poor alike. You said if one of the neighbors needed, the one that had would help. Aye Felipe, you produce such beautiful children, Felipito, Marialuisa and Vitorio. **(To Vitorio.)** You know, you have your mother's eyes. Jim Daniels you have brought greed with you. You changed my father from an honest man to a thief. To satisfy your greed, my husband and son became murderers. The evil is over. You two will pay. Estrella Moreno, I am sorry for the pain I have caused. I will also pay.

(Don Felipe accepts her words as a man condemned to death. Señor Daniels, however, reaches for Vitorio's old pistola on the table. Unthinking, Marialuisa grabs the knife resting next to her cup and drives it through the hand of Señor Daniels, pinning it the table.)

El Viento

It was done. The riders, all Mexicanos, knew that the Flores rancho belonged to the Señora and they remembered the times before Señor Daniels arrived. They obeyed her orders. The two men would hang. Alma's justice would be served. In the light of the midnight fire, Señora Flores spoke one last command.

Señora Flores

There is a man in prison whose only crime is that he told the truth. He must be freed.

El Viento

The church bells announced to the town that it was Sunday morning. While last week they mourned, they now called the town together. The horses and wagons brought dust, the people marched respectfully into the fast-filling church. Padre Seco, now neatly groomed, watched as Señora Flores and Marialuisa filled their customary pew. The murmur now was only slight when Vitorio and Estrella Moreno moved to occupy the seats of Don Felipe and Señor Daniels. Amalia shuffled slowly, not being a morning person, and in the absence of last week's excitement, moved groggily and complained about the starchiness of her Sunday dress.

Amalia

Pero Mamá, it itches.

El Viento

She curled up in her seat as the choir sang the ancient words of praise, "Bendito, Bendito, Bendito sea dios, los angeles cantan..." I could not contain myself. I found myself swirling and dancing through the windows, ruffling the hymnals, tickling the altar flowers and cooling the faces and necks of the seated worshipers. The church bells continued to ring and I entered the steeple, catching a rising note, I vaulted into the street. I returned to the church on the heels of a brown suited man, who although tired, walked hurriedly up the stairs. He adjusted his collar and together we pushed the door open. La Misa was in progress. Amalia was now sleeping. I could not resist placing a kiss on her beaded forehead. Cooled, she awoke as the humble congregation quieted to witness the return of a long lost son. The man spoke...

Papi

Mija, I'm home.

Amalia

(Amalia jumps from her seat and into his arms.) Papi, Papi, my Papi's home.

El Viento

The family sat, prayed and sang together, now proud, throughout the remainder of the mass. Afterwards, the church bells rang gloriously, announcing for miles the joyous reunion. As I made one last pass through the rapidly emptying church, Papi and Ana were accepting the well wishes of their friends and neighbors. I suddenly felt a tug on my tail that halted me immediately.

Amalia

I watched you this morning, you brought my Papi back.

El Viento

I watched her hands, strong and tiny. I smiled, but she would not release me from her grip.

Amalia

Thank you for bringing him to me. Before I let you go, will you promise to come back and play with me?

El Viento

I nodded, she released me, and I rose high above the town of Alma. I watched the town move and come alive as the comadres stood on the church steps and exchanged chisme. The compadres stood on the street corner and exchanged more chisme. **(El Viento lights a candle.)** This is the length of a human life, bright, warm and brief.

The flame, as fragile as the life that we hold in our hands. Remember the hands that are small. It is the little hands that reach for dreams. It is the little hands that cradle our hearts. It is little hands that hold the wind.

Fin

Vocabulary Section

Alma - soul
arroz de leche-rice with milk
bienvenidos-welcome
Bruja-witch
caldo-soup
campesino-peasant
canela-cinnamon
carpa-tent show
chisme-gossip
Chismosa-female gossip
Chismoso-male gossip
chocolaté-chocolate
conjunto- a band or style of music particular to South Texas
contesta-to answer
copal-incense
el pueblo esta de luto-the town is in mourning
El Viento-the wind
Hurucán-Mayan god who created the universe
Indita-female who has indian features
La misa de los pobres siempres-The mass of the eternal poor
La Virgen Chismosa-the gossiping virgen
lechusa-female owl
"me mataron"- "they killed me"
mija-an affectionate name for a child, literally my daughter
muchacho-boy
niño-a baby or a small child
Nuestra Señora de las Almas Perdidas-Our Lady of the Lost Souls
Papi-nickname for father
pero-but
por favor-please
pistola-pistol
pueblito-small town or village
quinceañera-a young girl's 15 birthday party, her coming out party
ranchito-a small ranch
rinches -derogatory name for Texas Rangers
San Antonio-Saint Anthony

The Day Ricardo Falcón Died

Picture from The Day Ricardo Falcón Died
Cast from left to right: Michael Marquez-Harp, Steve Pacheco, Susana
Cordova, Paul A. Zamora, Karen G. Stack, Alfonso Suazo, and Santo Alvarez

El Centro Su Teatro
presents
The Day Ricardo Falcon Died

written and directed by
Anthony J. Garcia

Assistant Director-Yolanda Ortega-Ericksen
Light & Sound-Leo Griep-Ruiz
Set Design-Joe Craighead
Costumes-Sherry Coca-Candelaria and Yolanda Ortega-Ericksen

Cast

The Old Folks
Miguel-Rich Beall
Luisa-Sherry Coca-Candelaria
Herman-Manuel Roybál
Louie-Angel Mendez-Soto
The Hispanics
Leti-Susana Córdova
Suzy-Sherry Coca-Candelaria
Las Limpiadoras
Maria-Susana Cordova
Juanita-Karen G. Slack
The Brothers
Pito-Santo Álvarez
Pata-Alfonso Suazo Jr.
The UMAS Students
Evelina-Susana Córdova
Miguel -Steve Pacheco
Oso-Michael Marquez-Harp
Raul-Santo Álvarez
Armando-Alfonso Suazo Jr.
Yolanda-Karen G. Slack
And Vern
Vern Gallegos-Paul A. Zámora

Children's Voices-Marcos Martinez and Olivia Martinez
Yo Soy Chicano sung by Debra Gallegos
Light Tech-Steve Nash & Roy Rodriquez
Sound Tech-Leo Griep-Ruíz

Music
American Pie-Don McLean
Viva Tirado Otra Vez-El Chicano
Brown Eyed Girl-(Morrison) El Chicano
Soul Sacrifice-Carlos Santana
Samba pa' ti-Carlos Santana
The Revolution will not be Televised-Gil Scott-Heron

Special thanks to Timothy Ferraro, George Manchauk, Susan Muldin,
Mary Smart, Rev. Kathy(Preacher Lady) Mitchell & Pilgrim
Congregational Church. Dan Garcia, Geraldina Lawson, KGNU, KUVO
89.3, Nathen Garcia, Marc & Caroline and Bobby Astorga.

Publicity photos by Daniel Salazar

The Ricardo Falcón Died
and Su Teatro's 20th Anniversary

In 1971, a group of university instructors, students and community activists began discussion about the effects teatros was having on the growing Chicano Movement and the movement for social change. Guerrilla companies such as the San Francisco Mime Troupe, Bread and Puppet Theatre, the Radical Arts Troupe and the Living Theater were proving to be valuable arms of the antiwar/anti-imperialist movement. For Chicanos, groups such as El Teatro Campesino (the Farmworkers Theater) El Teatro de la Esperanza (The Theater of Hope) and El Teatro de la Gente (The Theater of the People) were carrying a more specific and cultural message. The Chicano teatros had been influenced also by Mexican groups such as Los Mascarones (A mask theater group named for the carved masks worn in classical theater, a name that stayed after the radicalization of the company). Deciding this form of expression was needed, the founders would enter Su Teatro into the theater world.

I think in those days, performances were carried on the strength of the individual's personalities and the teatros constantly lost people to other areas of movement work. Very few of us thought that doing teatro would ever serve as a career. Many of us believed that the revolution would take place tomorrow and consequently our lives could only be planned so far in advance. But the revolution did not take place the next day. Somehow, Su Teatro has continued for 20 years and today is known as El Centro Su Teatro. Su Teatro still clings to the ties of the community and the struggle for social change. Su Teatro gas not and will not deny the radical fire that forged it s beginning. Su Teatro often take stands that will keep it from reaching the political and artistic mainstream. Su Teatro will bust it collective ass to provide the best production and artistic values it can.

People often want to know how it was at the beginning. For me, it was those middle years, the 1980's, the Reagan Years, the Disco years, "the decade of the Hispanic", that were the most difficult; it was the impetus for us to be here tonight. Many of them are still here, Rudy, Debra, Sherry, Angel and Yolanda. There are others. I thought at one time of trying to list everyone who has had a part of Su Teatro,

but the list would be too long and inevitable incomplete. People who have inspired me in the teatro are Rowena Rivera, Diana De Herrera-Garcia, Tep Falcón, Alfredo Sandoval, Kenny Binkley-Trujillo, Judy Sandoval and the aforementioned 5. I am sure other members have their list, but since
I am writing the program, my list will stand as the rule. I also want to thank the members of the 20th Anniversary Commitee, Aleta Abelman, Magdalena Gallegos, Kris Montoya and Alicia Ávila.

The Day Ricardo Falcón Died began as a short story written while I was working at El Teatro Campesino. I was given the opportunity of doing the reading as a one-act play. The play's final evolution occurred in between rewrites of, "Ludlow: El Grito de las Minas" .

My memories of the Chicano Movement are not of nostalgia, but of a sense of urgency, purpose and commitment. I remember Ricardo's death as a shocking awakening that the changing rules of a society was a game that was played for keeps. For me, it was a loss of innocence or naiveté. I realized how easily one of our own could be taken from us. I remember those who devoted their lives and families to that cause. Some sacrificed both. Nineteen years after Ricardo Falcón's death, we are still going through a healing process. We have not allowed ourselves to mourn properly those who correctly or incorrectly exhibited the highest level of commitment to their families and to their people. As I was writing, I asked myself which leaders would be willing to challenge the state to that level today? I asked this question of myself, but could not give not answer convincingly enough. I then asked myself, what lessons can we give not only to our children, but to ourselves to deal with the realities of living on the Eve of the New World Order? The answer I heard was to look to our past, to look to our families and to remember the ideals, we had before we lost our innocence.

The Day Ricardo Falcón Died

Act One

(Music up to a dark stage. It is a modest urban Chicano home. The furniture is simple, not new but it once was. In the center of the room, directly across from the sofa is a color television with attached VCR, a high-tech stereo/compact disk player. Directly behind the sofa is a desk and a typewriter. It is set to divide the room and allow anyone working at the desk to view the television from the desk. The walls are arranged with contrasting paintings by Diego Rívera, posters by Malaquias Montoya and photographs of family members. To the right of the stage is a door that exits into the bedroom, against the back wall is another door, which is the front door of the house. Don McLean's *American Pie* is playing in background. Midway through the chorus, the record changes abruptly, including the scratching sound of a needle across a record. Music changes to *El Grito* by the musical group El Chicano. Lights up to a special on Miguel. He narrates as if he is writing a story.)

Miguel

"The old Mejicano was now a drunk. He stared, glassy eyed as the scene unfolded before him. (**An image appears on a riser upstage.**) Here was the woman he had married as a young girl, now worn and tired, her eyes sadly agonized with each ancient step. She cursed the house as if it contained a possessing spirit, damning it and all the misery it represented." (**Miguel pauses, images disappear, and he crumbles up the page from a legal notepad and tosses it aside.**) That's pretty depressing. Four sentences into the story and you want to kill yourself. I want something lighter...(**Another image appears.**) John was a barrio kid, he had once been a cop but his Mamá told him he should get a respectable job. Actually he left the force. No one knows why? He wouldn't say. Maybe he got tired of busting the Raza, maybe it was that he couldn't stand the racist system, maybe he didn't like the ugly white cars or the boots that made you walk like you had shit in your pants. But it didn't matter, because he was now "Johnny Chacón: Chicano Eye ". (**Johnny Chacón, low-slung PI hat across his face and a trench coat, turns to the audience and says..**)

Johnny Chacón

Eye te watcho.

Miguel

(Image disappears. Lights up in Migúel's living room. Miguel crumbles the paper once more.) Yeeech, now I know why they call it gag writing. **(Door to kitchen opens and Herman, Miguel's older brother, enters the living room eating a bowl of chile and beans. He kicks his way through the door with such a force that it startles Miguel.)**

Herman

Sorry carnal, I didn't know you were here.

Miguel

(Irritated.) Let me get this straight. You came by because you thought I might be gone?

Herman

(Nonplussed.) Not really.

Miguel

What did you think when you found the door was unlocked?

Herman

The door was unlocked? **(Pause.)** Sorry. I was hungry.

Miguel

Why don't you eat at home? That's why you married what's-her-face.....the gringa.

Herman

Her name is Christine, and you could make an effort to like her.

Miguel

I do make an effort **(Pause.)** at your house. But you're not at your house, you're at my house, eating my food.

77

Herman

I had to, Christine doesn't make beans and chile, especially beans and she hates it when I eat them, too.

Miguel and Herman

Because I fart.

Miguel

So you come to my house to eat and fart.

Herman

Leave me alone man, I'm stressed.

Miguel

Look man, I warned you when you married her, that you only cared about two things **(Pause.)** beans and chile. Really I don't care that she's white. You were lonely and divorced, and it's your life. But it's my house and my refrigerator. My only revenge is that the beans and chile are two weeks old.

Herman

(Herman shrugs and keeps eating) Speaking of relationships, where's Luisa? And don't lie to me, I can always tell, when you two are fighting. **(Holds up an empty beer he finds laying on the table.)**

Miguel

(Walks to phone and picks up an invitation.) This came in the mail.

Herman

Yeah? So what? I got one of those too. I thought it was a subpoena or something bad.

Miguel

Look who's sponsoring it. **(Herman has the same blank look on his face.)** Coors **(Herman doesn't react.)**

Coors beer.

Herman

First you complain about me eating your food and then you offer me a beer. I don't get it.

Miguel

I'm not joking man, after all the crap the Coors family has pulled on Chicanos and Blacks. Remember how lucky blacks should feel about being brought here in chains?

Herman

When?

Miguel

That's what the old man told a group of black leaders.

Herman

You take everything so serious. I'm going. "Little Joe" is playing. Come on man, you should go. I can't take those Hispanic things. When you go, at least I feel like I'm not the only Chicano there, and then we can make fun of people. Then I have a good time .

Miguel

Hell no, I ain't gonna go and be seen with those suckasses. And if you go, you aren't my brother.

Herman

You can't just make me not your brother.

Miguel

I'll put bars on the kitchen windows. I'll get a pitbull and tease him with your shorts, even though he might not live through the experience.

Herman

Is this why you and Luisa are fighting? She wants to go? **(Miguel doesn't say anything.)**

She sees those people in her job all the time, government bureaucrats, entrepreneurs, even unemployed contractors like me. We all go so we can circulate, find out what's happening, check out each other's old ladies. It's harmless.

Miguel

The Hispanic Agenda wants to shape the future with Coors' money. I think that is both hypocritical and dangerous. I hate Hispanic anything. I don't consider myself Hispanic. How many Spaniards came here to marry Indian women?

Herman

(Interrupting.) I don't know, four maybe?

Miguel

You're saying you don't care. Okay fine, just never mind.

Herman

No, no, please tell me. **(Pause.)** I really want to know, en serio.

Miguel

What I call myself is how my children identify themselves. If I let someone call me a greaser or a spic, then my children believe that we have no power to stop racism. On the other hand, if I say that I am Spanish-American or Hispanic because I want to be more European and deny the Indian part of us, then I am lying to myself and everyone else.

Herman

What? You don't think I look Spanish.

80

Miguel

Yeah, you look like the fat sergeant that Zorro used to beat up. Realistically, even if somewhere way back, one of our ancestors was Spanish, that doesn't mean that they married other Spaniards after that. Besides, our family is from New Mexico, nothing but cattle and sheep and the four Spaniards who came over to marry Indian women.

Herman

This is why you and Luisa are fighting? Over Zorro, Spaniards and the sheep.

Miguel

Well, she wants to go to this thing to be seen. I don't want to go. So that's the fight.

Herman

What's the problem? Why doesn't she just go without you? You've done that before right?

Miguel

Yeah but,

Herman

But you don't want her to go.

Miguel

I would prefer that she choose not to go.

Herman

And so you're disappointed in her for not making the choice that you wanted her to make.

Miguel

She can choose anything she wants but,

Herman

But?

Miguel

But every choice has consequence.

Herman

So you want Luisa to have choices, as long as they are the correct choices. She is independent up to a certain point, where she doesn't cross you. Right?

Miguel

Why the hell are you psychoanalyzing me? Did Oprah have a two-parter on "machismo in relationships"? Why don't you look at yourself? You're so pussy whipped, you sneak over to my house to eat beans and chile because you're afraid to fart in your own house. Why do you suddenly know the answers to all my problems?

Herman

Because I feel the same way. If you give women too many choices, not only will they pick the exact opposite of what you want, but they'll take forever to do it. You ever see one buy a pair of shoes? Every shoe in the store is taken out before they pick the first pair they looked at.

Miguel

Why am I even talking to you? You're still going to the dance. You're going because your wife, the gring-ahhh...(**Miguel catches himself.**) Christine, is a liberal. She has ordered you to go, and you are such a wimp you give into her because you know you'll never get laid again if you don't do what she says.

Herman

True, but I'm weak. You don't have the same expectations from me as you do from others. (**Picking up Miguel's manuscript from desk.**) So how's the writing? (**Miguel snatches the script back.**) That bad huh? (**Takes out his wallet.**) So how you doing for money? (**Places

a twenty on the table.) Big brother guilt.

Miguel

(Takes the twenty and takes the manuscript from Herman's hands.) You still can't see it. **(He throws manuscript into the trash can.)** It's crap anyway.

Herman

When's your deadline?

Miguel

Last week. I spent the advance, I missed the deadline and my girlfriend is leaving me. You want a beer?

Herman

Seems to me that you need to write.

Miguel

How about cards on Friday? I'll have beans and chile.

Herman

Let me check with Christine.

Miguel

You're such a wuss. Come on, just the guys. You can even bring that idiot buddy of yours.

Herman

You mean Louie?

Miguel

Yeah, stupidity looking for a place to happen.

Herman

Are you going to pick on him?

Miguel

Absolutely.

Herman

Okay, maybe. **(Starts to exit.)** 'bye. **(Stops at the door).** Call Mom, okay? You don't call and she bitches me out.

Miguel

Well, you're the oldest, accept some responsibility. **(Pause.)** Grab me a beer. **(Miguel goes to the typewriter and puts a new sheet of paper in. Herman returns and puts the beer next to him.)**

Herman

Why don't you get a computer like everyone else?

(Miguel gives him a look of disapproval.) Okay. Later. **(He exits.)**

Miguel

(Miguel begins to write.) She looked lost amid the shuffle of the railway station. **(An image appears upstage. It is a young woman.)** A lonely lost woman-child. Yet, there was a look of determination on her face. She had come to the border town to make contact with the Americanos who were willing to back her people's cause. After months of hiding out in the hills with the Villistas, she had been asked to call upon her finishing school upbringing to charm the Americanos, to show them that the revolution had sophistication and was not just a peasant movement. Funny, she thought, how much more sophisticated the peasants were than the Americano bankers, who saw the revolution as an opportunity to bet both sides. Naturally, they would give twice as much to the Diaz regime.

Yasmín

(Taking her hair down and removing her starched collar the image speaks to Miguel.) Why can't I just be a peasant woman, or just a mother trying to raise her children? Why do I have to be a sophisticated revolutionary, or the treacherous hooker working in the cantinas? Why don't you make me what I am?

Miguel

(Miguel replies to image.) Why do you have to fight with me? Can't you ever just do as I say?

Yasmín

Whose story is it anyway?

Miguel

Mine. **(Pause.)** Okay, but can't we just once try it my way?

Yasmín

(Exasperated.) Sure. Let's go.

Miguel

Jezabela, looked for a familiar face in the crowd.

Yasmín

(Image takes on the persona of the character.) Wait a minute, hold it.

Miguel

What, now?

Yasmín

Jezabela? What kind of a name is Jezabela?

Miguel

It was my grandmother's name.

Yasmín

Don't impose biblical morality. You may as well call me a tramp. I don't like it.

Miguel

How about Josefina?

Yasmín

Not bad, but plain.

Miguel

I thought you wanted me to be an ordinary woman?

Yasmín

But that doesn't mean I want an ordinary name.

Miguel

(Miguel begins writing again. Image takes on the personality of the character he writes about.) She was an ordinary woman, with an extraordinary name, a name to match her flair, her determination and her dedication. Her mother had been given a love for books, and from the books she gave her daughter education and the name Yasmín.

Yasmín

Ooh, Jasmina, I like that. What's next?

Miguel

I don't know? That's all I got.

Yasmín

Well think harder.

Miguel

That's all I got. Pretty girl, railroad station and then blank. Sorry. **(Phone rings and Miguel picks it up, image huffs offstage.)**

Hello. Yeah, this is Miguel. Armando, I haven't heard from you in years, how's the family? David Padilla? Yeah, I remember him. The funeral is tomorrow? Did he suffer long? That quickly huh?.

One day you're here and the next day you're gone. Yeah. I'll be there.

(**Miguel hangs up phone, opens the can of beer and takes a big drink. Lights down. Up on three figures, two females and one male. The three are at a podium and are dressed in formal attire.**)

Manny Diaz

(**Applause.**) Good evening everyone and welcome to our annual awards dance and salute. You might not recognize the two lovely ladies next to me. They are Leti Olivares-Cummings and Suzy Maldonado-Lewis.

Suzy

Manny, tonight we are here to raise money for the Hispanic Liposuction and Cosmetic Surgery Institute. Manny, many people don't realize that Hispanics also suffer from obesity and ugliness. This is a good safe charity and gives us a chance to pat ourselves on the back, just like the white people do.

Leti

Many people, like Manny and Suzy, suffer feelings of inferiority because they don't have access to advanced cosmetic medicine. Upwardly mobile competition can often be brutal for the Hispanic who believes that opulence is a right.

Manny

It makes no sense to drive to a country club in a BMW, if you can't fit into it. Suzy, by the way, I really like your lift, isn't it wonderful folks? (**Applause.**) Someday it is our hope that Hispanics, moving into the upper income levels, won't have to wait for that tax shelter to pay off.

Leti

That's right Manny. Suzy, here, was starting to crinkle. A little crow's feet, a little drooping on the chin. Suzy and I however are fortunate. We're married to white guys with money. Last year, Suzy's face had enough lines to be a map of the new highway configuration, but this year Suzy you look beautiful. (**Applause.**)

Suzy

Thank you, Leti. I can see you added a little more body to those sagging old "32's" you've been passing off a breasts. **(Ladies start to go back and forth insulting each other.)**

Manny

Ladies, let's move on. Let's not forget why we're here,

Leti

Manny don't be so high and mighty. Everyone knows you got this year's cute buns to replace last year's fat ass. **(She gooses him, Manny jumps.)**

Manny

Stop it, I haven't gotten the stitches out. **(Realizing where he is, he regains his composure).** Tonight, we are here to honor a man, and tears well up in my eyes, **(Massages his butt.)** whose contributions are many. They represent the progress of the Hispanic community. Where once stood radicals and social causes, we now have moderates, conservatives and social calendars. This man, I have to tell you, has proven himself to be an adequate political chameleon. First denying any Hispanic connection, then immersing himself, at least partially, in **(Indicates quotation marks.)** "his culture" when he realized it was advantageous to do so, while never forgetting to wrap himself in the flag. Hispanos and Hispanas, Gring-ohs and Gring-ahs, I give you Vern Gal-egg-ohs.

(Scene returns to the inside of Miguel's house. Herman enters from kitchen, he is talking to someone in the kitchen. Miguel is asleep on the couch but Herman does not see him.)

Herman

Don't panic I've done this a bunch of times with my wife. Just relax and drink your beer. I'll put some music on. **(In a lilting voice.)** Don't go away. **(Turns music up real loud.)**

Miguel

(Miguel jumps up screaming.) Vern, their honoring Vern. No, No!
(His scream startles Herman, who in turn screams, this brings
Louie out of the kitchen. Louie enters with his hair full of
curlers. Miguel screams, Louie screams, Herman orders Louie
back in the kitchen.)

Louie

What's going on in here?

Herman

I thought I told you to stay in the kitchen?

Louie

Yeah, but...(He looks at Miguel and then at Herman.) Okay.
(Starts to leave)

Miguel

No wait.

Louie

But he said...(Looks at Herman and then at Miguel.) Okay. (He
stays.)

Miguel

(To Herman.) What the hell's going on here?

Herman

(Nonchalant.) Nothing.

(Miguel looks at Louie.)

Louie

(Trying to match Herman's level of defiance.)   Nothing.
(Chickening out.) Okay. I'm going into the kitchen.

Herman

(To Louie.) Wait.

Louie

Okay.

Herman

You knocked one of your curlers out. Come here and sit down.
(Herman and Louie move to dining room table and Herman re-
curls the strand of hair. To Miguel. I thought you were going to be
out this afternoon?

Miguel

I was, I'm back now. (He looks at Louie.) And what are you doing?

Louie

My hair.

Herman

It was my idea. Louie wanted, you know, a special look for the dance on
Saturday.

Miguel

Damn! I'm sick of hearing about that pinche dance.

Herman

You look pretty dressed up. (Laughs) Somebody die?

Miguel

As a matter of fact they did. **(Grabs a beer that was sitting on the table, opens it and starts to take a drink. Louie starts to stop him but it is too late, Miguel takes a drink and spits it out.)** This damn beer is hot.

Louie

I forgot to put it in the fridge.

Miguel

What are you guys doing here?

Herman

It's Friday. Don't you remember? The card game, just the guys? Who died?

Miguel

A friend from a long time ago, you don't know him. His name was David Padilla.

Herman

Yeah sure. **(Indicates muscles.)** One of your radical friends. What happened?

Miguel

Heart attack... **(Snaps his finger.)** just like that. Cards huh? **(Looks at Louie.)** You got money?

Louie

(Proudly pats his pocket.) Just cashed my paycheck.

Miguel

(To Herman.) Okay.

(Door opens. Luisa enters with her brothers. The brothers are bulked-up dimwits, who are dressed like they just stepped out of

91

the worst gang movie imaginable. **She stops to look at Miguel but moves past him.)** I just came by to pick up some clothes for the dance tomorrow night.

Miguel

(Moves to talk to her.) So you're still going huh? **(Brothers move to protect Luisa who exits to bedroom.)** Don't start. I don't want to get stupid-punk-blood all over my carpet. **(Miguel notices their sports caps or jackets.)** When did being an idot become a sport?

Pito

(To Louie with threatening tone.) Would you rather have us run around in curlers, Louie?

Miguel

Hey leave him alone. He doesn't have to answer to you.

Louie

(To Miguel.) I don't?

Miguel

(Indicating Pito) No, he's too stupid to formulate questions.

Louie

Miguel, you're sticking up for me?

Miguel

Shut up Louie, and take those stupid curlers out of your hair.

(Louie moves towards the kitchen.)

Pito

Why doesn't everybody just stay in here. I don't want you bringing weapons in from the kitchen.

Herman

Look, when you're at your house you can give orders. But right now
we're at my house. I mean his house. **(Indicates Miguel.)**

Miguel

(To Pito.) Hey, fuck you. **(Starts to move to Pito and his brother.
Herman and Louie move in to join the confrontation. Luisa
enters carrying a box of clothes. She is unaware of the
confrontation taking place.)**

Luisa

Can someone help me with this box? **(She thrusts it into Miguel's
belly, who does the same to Pito. Pito gives him a threatening
look. Miguel smiles.)**

Miguel

You came to help.

Luisa

(Indicating Miguel's tie.)

How did they get you to put one of these things on? Somebody die?

Miguel

Yeah.

Luisa

(Taken aback.) Oh.

Miguel

Don't worry about it. It's no one you know.

Luisa

Just the same, I'm sorry.

Miguel

You are?

Luisa

About your friend, I mean.

Miguel

It happens. I'm okay.

Luisa

(Emotions between Miguel and Luisa are building.) Okay.

Miguel

Are you okay? **(He touches her on the shoulder. They look at each other for a moment and jump into each others arms. They kiss each other passionately, she wraps her legs around him and they fall to the ground behind the couch. Everyone watches in amazement.)**

Herman

(Moving threateningly to Pito and his brother.) I think you better go. **(The brothers turn and exit. After a moment Herman glances behind the couch and realizes Miguel and Luisa aren't stopping. He says to Louie.)** I think we better go.

Louie

What about my hair? **(They exit.)**

(Lights down. Music up, *"Dicen que es el año del Chicano"*. Sound of rain falling in the background.)

Young Miguel

(He inhales from a cigarette and chokes on it.) Shit. **(He throws it down and crushes it under his foot.)** I walked through the fog as if I were blindfolded, waving my hands in front of me, fearful of what I had just passed, terrified at what I might encounter. The summer rain forced the tear gas ever so slowly to the ground. My eyes burned. My tears had torn streaks down my face. My face burned. The rain muddied the streets, the streets burned. The sirens sliced like flashing switchblades through the night. The night burned. A cop dragged a young girl by her hair to the paddy wagon. and my soul burned. My heart screamed and my eyes teared once again. The world revealed itself to me the night. And, for the first time I faced it and shouted, "Ya basta".

(Crossfade to interior of house, Mejicana cleaning ladies enter.)

Maria

Ay Juanita, esta es tu primera noche, y yo te voy a enseñar las reglas del trabajo. Estás lista? Quedate aquí conmigo y yo te enseño todo. Bueno la primera cosa es que nunca pero nunca dejes que los gringos ni peor todavia los patrones, te oigan hablar en inglés. Porque si saben que hablas en inglés van a querer que hablas mas y ya que hablas mas inglés van a querer mas trabajo, y mira , mujercita hay mucho. Ah pues, a mi me gusta escucharlos hechar con su español. Yo una vez, tenia un patron con el cuello todo torcido, tratando de decir "ere" nada mas. Pues no hablas mucho eh, Juanita?

Juanita

Si.

Maria

No como la Carmen, con quíen trabajaba antes, huy la Carmen era tremenda. Tu crees que yo hablo, pues no, la Carmen, o pués, ya no está con nosotros. Ella firmó una peticíon del sindicato, pués del únion, y el patrón se latero y la corrio, ay pués, la pobre Carmen, tenia cuatro hijos. Tu tienes hijos?

Juanita

Si.

Maria

Pos cuanto?

Juanita

Siete.

Maria

Híjole! Siete! Pues yo tengo tres. Yo le dije a mi Ramon, le dije, sabes que? Cada vez que yo te cargo por quince minutos, cargo tu hijo por nueve meses, la siguiente vez que tu quieres un hijo, tu eres el que va a cargar y nos quedamos con tres. **(Pause.)**

Pos cuanta gente crees que estará aqui en la noche?

Juanita

Cinquenta?

Maria

Cinquenta! No, pués, mucho mas, mucho mas, es un baile de los Hispanics. Sabes que son los Hispanics, que no? Son Mejicanos que quieren ser Republicans pero no tienen suficiente dinero. Se van a dar premios a si mismo. Que raro, verdad? Si. Pués estamos listos, que no? La mesa, los vasos, el ponche. Se van a entrar por aquí, todos bíen vestidos. Los hombres, bien guapos y las mujeres, bien bonitas y nos miraran, no? Con estos ojos que dicen que bueno que yo no soy tu. Y nosotros les daremos de comer y de cenar.

Y ellos nos hecharon fumo en la cara y despúes, limpiaremos y ellos nunca, nunca nos darán las gracias.

Juanita

Maria?

Maria

Huh? Ah pués callate mujer, aqui toma. **(Gives Juanita a glass of punch. She turns to audience and raises her glass, smiling. She speaks humbly in heavily accented, broken English.)** I would like to thank everybody for giving me this prize, for Juanita y mi. Pues it has been a long time that nobody never did notice what we been doing here, and I been here, pues longer than I could remember. Who knew that when we were little girls cleaning that we would be training for a career, verdad?

Juanita

Si.

Maria

Si. Pero most of all, I would like to thank mi familia. Mi Ramón, y mis hijitos for being here tonight, muchisimas gracias, for being proud of your Mama! Salúd!

(Maria & Juanita finish off their punch. Juanita is getting nervous about not working. She pats Maria on the arm to signal her to go. Maria takes one last moment.) Buenas noches. **(She stops and nudges Juanita, encouraging her to accept the applause. Juanita does so. Vern Gallegos enters and seeing the Mejicanas, he gives them a stern look, and they move to leave.)** Juanita, you probably think I'm crazy?

Juanita

Si. (They exit)

(Blackout. Music by "Little Joe y la Familia" is heard.)

Announcer

(From off stage.)

Ladies and gentlemen, Little Joe y la Familia.

(Miguel, Herman and Louie enter. Others enter behind them bringing a punch bowl and decorations. Louie's hair is plastered to his head, the results of the failed perm attempt. Miguel is noticeably drunk. Music ends. Herman exits briefly and re-enters.)

Herman

Okay I bribed the guy who plays the music while the band is on break.

Miguel

Good. Then he'll do it? **(Music up. Texas Tornados, "Hey baby que paso")** Okay...the fat guy dance.

(Miguel, Herman and Louie stick their bellies out of their shirts and begin to dance disgustingly to the music. Luisa, sees the spectacle they are making and moves to intervene.)

Luisa

(Quietly to Miguel.) Miguel, don't do this to me.

Miguel

(Trying to dance with her.) Hey baby, que paso? I thought I was your only vato.

Luisa

Miguel stop it, you're drunk.

Miguel

Not completely.

Luisa

You're making a fool of yourself.

Miguel

Not completely. **(Sees someone he doesn't like.)**

Hey look an Hispanic state senator, the man who is afraid to defend an affirmative action program that gave him his first job. **(He laughs.)** Watch me scare the politicians, "quotas, quotas, quotas." Isn't it amazing how, twenty years into the civil rights movement, the racists are calling civil rights racist. And the politicians who got their jobs because of the movement, are afraid to offend the racists. Vote for me I'm a chickenshit.

(Vern Gallegos has been working the crowd and seeing the confrontation, with teeth flashing comes to introduce himself. He has been eyeing Luisa.)

Vern

Hi, Vern Gallegos, here. (Presents a business card and extends his hand to Miguel. Miguel ignores him.)

Miguel

Speaking of chickenshits. I gotta take leak. (He turns to exit, as Vern and Luisa, who are more familiar with each other than they pretend, move to the side to talk. Miguel begins pissing in the punchbowl.)

Vern

Your friend seems a little out of it. Maybe somebody should take him home.

Luisa

But then I would be alone.

Vern

Then I suppose I'll have to take you home. I spoke to the others on the committee, they are just as impressed with you as I am, Luisa. I would say that an appointment is a strong possibility.

Luisa

That's great Vern. I really want to be in a situation where I can impact change.

(Miguel returns with three cups of punch, all of which are spilling over. He has overheard the conversation.)

Vern

Speaking of changing, you left these. (Vern holds up a pair of panties. Luisa is shocked as Vern returns to the conversation.)

The room is filled with Hispanicity, isn't it?

Miguel

(Showing irritation because he has been interrupted.) Yes. Isn't it wonderful. **(Feigned familiarity.)** Vern, right?

Vern

Yes. Vern Gallegos.

Miguel

I may have been a little rude a second ago, but I had to go take a leak real badly. Being a guy, you know how that goes. Here let's have a toast. **(Offers a drink to Vern and Luisa.)** You know, I think I may have had too much to drink. **(Throws the drink over his shoulder and holds an empty glass.)** To friends. **(Squeezes Vern's shoulder whom he has been hugging. They drink).** And lovers. **(Squeezes Luisa. They drink.)** To overheard conversations and **(Everyone raises their glasses.)** panties in our pockets. **(Luisa and Vern all stop in mid-drink.)** No don't stop. Drink up my friends. **(Luisa and Vern finish their glasses.)**

Vern

Thank you for the drink, I think I'll be... **(Miguel doesn't release him.)**

Luisa

Let him go, Miguel.

Miguel

Luisa, a tooth gets impacted, people and situations don't. Bureaucrats should not be allowed to tamper with the language. The word you wanted was to "affect" change. You could even say, "make change", or "change things". I know what you're thinking. You're thinking that I should implement some damage control. Why don't you just tell me to shut my mouth.

Luisa

Miguel, shut your mouth.

Miguel

See you can return to the vernacular. Talk like a person, it turns me on.

Vern

Maybe you two should be alone.

Miguel

What's the matter Vern? Is it the bureaucratic talk that gets your pecker wagging? Did you two network or did you screw?

Luisa

How can you wave the flag of fidelity?

Miguel

I can't, that's why I did your cousin last summer.

Luisa

You son-of-a-bitch.

Vern

People are watching you fight.

Miguel

No Vern. They are perceiving a potentially, near life-threatening confrontational situation. You wanted her Vern are you afraid to fight for her?

Luisa

Now you come to life, Miguel. Your most valued possession is being threatened.

Miguel

I wouldn't call you my most valuable.

Luisa

I meant your male ego, you asshole. **(Luisa slaps him. Miguel turns to Luisa. Vern spins him around and sneakers him. Herman steps in to defend Miguel. Vern is too quick, punches Herman and knocks him into Louie. Miguel gets up and punches Vern. Luisa grabs the punch bowl and pours the punch on Miguel's head. Music up. Blackout.)**

Act II

Scene I

(Lights up in Manuel's living room. There is an anxious knock at the door. Miguel enters lazily from the bedroom, he is still in his jockey shorts, he calls out....

Miguel

Hang on a sec, I'm coming. (Miguel pushes back the curtain, and recognizes Louisa waiting. He opens the door, letting it continue opening on its' own. He crosses to sit on the couch. Luisa enters.) Why didn't you use your own key?

Luisa

Aren't you even going to say, "Hello"?

Miguel

(Sighs.) Good morning.

Luisa

No it's not. I don't remember where I left them.

Miguel

Boy, you've been leaving lots of things lying around, keys, panties...(Pause.)...and me.

Luisa

Look who's talking. (Angry.) You've been dropping your pants every time I turn my back. (Looking at Miguel, Luisa becomes serious.) How does it feel, when the shoe's on the other foot, hon?

Miguel

(Genuinely sad.) It hurts like hell.

103

Luisa

(Luisa not hiding her tears, sniffles and kisses Miguel passionately. She then pulls herself away from him and looks Miguel straight in the eyes.) I'm leaving you Miguel.

Miguel

I figured as much. It's been three months. (Looking at his watch.) You were due.

Luisa

You're such an asshole.

Miguel

And you're a flake. (He walks into the kitchen, re-enters with a beer and an egg. He drops the egg into the glass, pours beer into the glass and takes a drink. After struggling to hold the swallow down, he belches and smiles at Luisa.)

Luisa

(Exits to the bedroom in disgust. She returns with Miguel's robe and tosses it to him.) Here.

Miguel

But you like me in these shorts, you bought them for me.

Luisa

They fit then.

Miguel

(Boasting.) Are you saying that I've grown?

Luisa

No Miguel, I'm saying you're not the same person.

(Miguel puts the robe on. Luisa exits to the bedroom once again and this time returns with a suitcase of clothes and assorted personal items. She throws items from the living room into the suitcase.)

Luisa

I'll have my brothers come by to pick up the rest of my things.

Miguel

Tell them not to take the typewriter this time.

Luisa

That's right, without the typewriter the great Chicano masterpiece will continue to lie dormant. Why don't you get a computer like everyone else.

Miguel

Que cabrona! You've been hanging around me too long. And to think, you once said such sweet things.

Luisa

I don't need your help to articulate. Anyway, I'll have my brothers pick up my bookcase and my desk.

Miguel

You gave me the bookcase and the desk--that time you left to live with your old boyfriend. Never mind, llevatelos.

Luisa
It's better if your not around when my brothers come by.

Miguel

This is my house. If your brothers don't like it they can get fucked. What? Is your Pa gonna show up with a shotgun and string me up for messin' with his kin? I'm not going to run and hide.

Luisa

You should, you do a good snake.

Miguel

Look, Herman and I will drop off your stuff. Besides, I thought hillbilly families beat up boyfriends when the daughter was pregnant and he had to get married?

Luisa

Do you want to get married?

Miguel

I thought you were leaving?

Luisa

You're answering my question with a question.

Miguel

Do you want to get married?

Luisa

Another question.

Miguel

I'm not your type, anyway. I am not upwardly mobile enough. I'm not an Hispanic.

No, you're pathetic. Face facts, you're still looking for the dark-skinned, dark-eyed, Chicana militant, with her bandalera slung tight across her chi-chis, willing to die for Aztlán and her man, not necessarily in that order.

Miguel

Did you fuck Vern Gallegos?

Luisa

I would have to leave the country, to find a spot where you haven't laid your work. And God knows what you did when you went to school that year in Mexico. **(Pause.)** Quit grinning, you son-of-a-bitch. You hurt me.

Miguel

I'm sorry.

Luisa

You embarrassed me.

Miguel

I'm sorry. I didn't want to go to that dance but you insisted. You know I hate those people.

Luisa

Those people are my friends.

Miguel

Those people are scum. A bunch of pretty vendidos trying to see if they can out-gringo the gringo. Their Hispanic Agenda is a God-damn joke. They are all managers, bureaucrats and petty capitalists types, looking at how best to turn the poor into docile stiffs for their corporate bosses.

Luisa

Can the rhetoric.

Miguel

Because it's rhetoric doesn't mean it's not true. Really, tell me about where they talk about worker's rights, land rights, language freedom, or the need to maintain our identities as Chicanos. If you're gonna eat their power breakfast, why don't you ask them to serve up some huevos.

Luisa

They talk about jobs, for your precious working class.

Miguel

They want to create more wage-slaves so that they can become the new masters. Those people are Democrats in brown skin. Hell, those people are Republicans in brown skin.

Luisa

It doesn't change the fact that you got drunk.

Miguel

I'm sorry.

Luisa

You disrupted the keynote speaker.

Miguel

I'm sorry.

Luisa

You pissed in the punch.

Miguel

You're right **(Pause.)** and you screwed Vern Gallegos.

Luisa

You've got all the answers.

Miguel

I thought, I just had all the questions.

(Long pause. Luisa is crying softly. Miguel moves closer to touch her.)

Luisa

Don't touch me. **(Pause.)** Look, I'm going to stay over at my sister's until I can figure out what it is I want to do. Call before you drop off my stuff, I don't want to be there. **(She kisses him.)**

Miguel

Anything you say.

Luisa

Look at that. He finally gives a direct reply and it's conciliatory and patronizing. Miguel, cabron, last night you bragged about sleeping with my prima, not once, but all through our entire relationship. Aren't you proud of yourself? Wasn't I good enough for you? **(She heads to the door and stops to throws the invitation at him.)** Here's a souvenir for you. **(Luisa exits leaving the door ajar.)**

Miguel

(Miguel rushes to the door and yells out at her.) Tell Vern to send me your panties. If you get the desk, I want the panties. **(He returns to the living room and picks up the invitation, crumbles it and throws it at the television set. He begins tossing anything he can get his hands on across the room in a tantrum. He screams)** God damn it! **(He puts his head in his hands but doesn't cry. He goes to his desk drawer and begins searching for something. He piles papers on the desk from the drawer until he pulls out a photograph. The photograph is a group of 1960s Chicano college students, with raised arms and clenched fists. One of the students does not have his arm raised.)**

Vern Gal-egg-ohs, you son-of-a-bitch. It must only be the good who die young. You right-wing, racist, sexist, God-Bless-America-Asshole, you finally got me. **(He pushes everything off the desk and finding a sheet of paper in the heap, he inserts it into the typewriter and begins to type.)**

On a hot August day, the red sun melted in the west behind the green Colorado mountains. It was the thirtieth day of that month, thirty minutes remained till nightfall would swallow the last golden drops of the summer light.

I was sixteen, having graduated from high school a year early, I was a child among elders. Although the sun was setting on that summer of 1972. It nonetheless, was the spring of the Chicano Movement, a national movement aimed at the re-assertion of our identity as a Mestizo people, a movement to gain political, economic and social rights long denied us in the United States. **(Lights go up on the upper level of the stage to reveal a small office. Evelina, a Chicana of twenty-one, long black hair, black eyes, wearing jeans and a Mexican blouse is looking through a file cabinet. Oso, a heavy set muscular, imposing, bearded and long-haired Chicano is talking on the phone. The third person in the office has a green military fatigue jacket. He is somewhat light skinned, short-haired, his hair in contrast to the style of the day. He wears horn-rimmed glasses which harden his looks. The character is Vern Gallegos. Evelina is looking through the file cabinet. Oso is on the phone and Vern is smoking a cigarette with his feet up on his desk.)**

Miguel

"I entered the UMAS office. That is the United Mexican American Students office located in the downtown library building of the university. Carlos Santana is, "Soul Sacrificing" on the radio. Oh, hang on just a second. **(He moves into the kitchen, comes out with a beer. During this time, Oso, Evelina and Vern have frozen in their respective positions. Miguel returns and they start to move again. Miguel remembers something and snaps his fingers.)** Just one more thing.

(**Miguel runs to the stereo and pours through his record collection. He throws records over his shoulder as he digs and finally pulls out Santana's,** *Abraxas* **album. He puts the record on the turntable and cranks it up.** *Soul Sacrifice* **begins to play)** Much better. (**He seats himself at the typewriter, places a fresh sheet of paper in the typewriter)** Estan listos, entonces ya, comensamos.

(**The Chicano characters begin to move once more, lights down on the living room.**)

Oso

(**Talking on the phone**)

If the shit comes down, I don't want you cherrying out.

Vern

(**Checking out Evelina's ass as she bends over the filing cabinet**). Evelyn, you can sure file with the best of them.

Evelina

Why don't you shove it, marano.

Vern

You just tell me where.

Evelina

Vern, you make me sick. You think Chicanas are just for screwing. You don't have any respect, all you can do is make filthy remarks. But when I see you hanging around your skinny gringa girlfriends, you act happy if they just let you get close enough to smell it.

Oso

(**Looking up from the phone, laughing.**) She nailed your ass good, Vern. (**Going back to the phone.**) Yeah, we got three vans going.

Vern

David Padilla, boy revolutionary. C'mon Bear, you were in 'Nam. You know what it was like. **(To Evelina.)** Anytime you want to know, what a man does in a real combat situation, I'll be glad to show you.

(Young man enters carrying books. He is quiet and somewhat shy. He is the young Miguel. Vern sees him as he enters and begins to shift conversation to him.)

Vern

Hey Mikey, how you doing squid ?

Evelina

Callete el hocico, Vern don't call him that.

Vern

Mike, you know, once I had this gook hooker tie herself in a basket. Her pimps would twist the rope, then they would lower her onto you and when they released the rope....

Young Miguel

Hi, Evelina. **(Very shy about talking to her.)**

Evelina

Que huvo, Miguel. You going with us to El Paso?

Vern

Damn, those gook broads know how to make you feel like a man.

Evelina

Is that what you think a man is? Is that what makes you feel like a man? You sick piece of slime.

Young Miguel

El Paso? What's in El Paso? **(She doesn't hear him.)**

Oso

(Looking up from the phone he speaks to Miguel.) La Raza Unida convention. **(Returning to his phone conversation.)** Look, we want you guys with us, but if you guys are holding dope, you better tell us in case any shit comes down, we can dump it. **(Pause.)** Yeah, dump it. Don't tell me that shit over the phone. Shit. **(Puts his hand over the phone.)** Goddamn Eastsiders. **(Back to the phone.)** Yeah, that's why I'm the head of security.

Young Miguel

When is all this coming down?

Vern

Tomorrow night is the first night. They're leaving this afternoon. We can have the office all to ourselves, Mikey. Remember that night you got drunk at Ralph's, in the middle of a terrible snowstorm. Yeah, we got pretty close that night. You told me a lot of things, there Mikey. **(Vern gestures to Evelina who is now rolling up her sleeping bag and doesn't notice.)** You were very poetic. **(Miguel looks helplessly as Vern continues.)** Her perfectly round breasts grew larger with each passing breath.

Miguel

(Special up on older Miguel, he has changed out of his robe.) Oh Vern, shut up. That's not what I said.

(Actors freeze-except the younger Miguel.)

Young Miguel

You're the only one who can make him stop. **(Turns to Evelina.)** She's so beautiful.

Miguel

Yes, I remember. "Her brown eyes were singed with the fire of the sun. Her long black hair flowed as a river, past her naked neck, and with each succeeding breath, her brown breasts grew larger, or was that my breasts, strained with excitement. I am not sure because my eyes could not avoid her. The crowds of people surrounding us would melt, into the walls, the walls evaporating into a watercolored surrealist image. Evelina would glance at me and hold me frozen in her eyes. Her full pink lips would part and she would say, "Gracias", then she would pause and with tremendous affection she would punctuate her statement, "Carnal".

Young Miguel

(Repeats.) Then she would pause and with tremendous affection, she would punctuate her statement, "Carnal".

Vern

(Laughing.) Boy Mikey, you sure let it all out that night.

Raul

(Enters carrying an armful of sleeping bags.) What's so funny, Vern, Evelina stabbed you in the face with a pen again?

Armando

(Carrying in supplies for the trip.) Don't look at it as a scar, look at it as plastic surgery. She just added a dimple. (Turns to Oso.) So how's the security shaping up.

Oso

Real good boss. I got the vatos from Meztizo Park, the Westside Brown Berets and the MECHA at Community College.

Armando

How many?

Oso

Thirteen.

Vern

Sounds lucky. **(Laughs in Miguel's direction.)**

Younger Miguel

(Attempting to change the subject.) Armando, will Falcón be there? At the convention, I mean.

Vern

Ricardo Falcón?

Armando

Yeah, he's scheduled to address the conference general assembly.

Raul

He left last night.

Oso

(To Armando.) What's the housing situation?

Armando

There is an old church in the barrio willing to let us use their basement.

Raul

Two hundred sweaty bodies in a crowded church basement, sounds like fun.

Vern

Sounds like roaches.

Raul

(Menacing.) Sounds like you should shut up.

Vern

(Matching anger). Why don't you run out and get a beer pitcher, Ralph, your chickenshit, cheap shot put me in the hospital.

Raul

(Approaching Vern.) That's too bad, Vern, I was trying to kill you.

Vern

(Standing to challenge Raul.) I handled specks of shit like you everyday in 'Nam.

Armando

(Backing up Raul). That's spick, Vern, not speck. What are you doing here with us roaches anyway? Why don't you go hang out with the white rats?

Vern

Because my last name is Gal-egg-ohs and I have a right. This program is set up for those of us with Spanish surnames. It doesn't make any mention of radical politics.

Oso

(Intervening.) Look if you got to stay, keep it quiet. Raul, did you get the University van?

Raul

Yeah, and I got a station wagon, too. It's got a great tape deck in it, mood music (To no one in general.) tu sabes?

(The students go back to work. A special goes back up on the older Miguel. He is sitting on the couch and looking through old newspaper clippings.)

Older Miguel

Ricardo Falcón had spoken to the UMAS general membership two nights earlier. The effect had been inspiring. Falcón already was a campus legend. He grew up in a small rural Colorado town and recruited Chicanos from farmworking families onto the campus. He was one of us. He fought for us daily and when the university tried to fire him, we fought to get his job back. He spoke with compassion. He was fearless and after beating the university, we thought him to be invulnerable. **(Phone rings.)** Hello? Herman? What's up bro? What do you mean I sound bummed? Yeah Luisa left me, again. Yeah, I need to borrow your truck. Look I don't want to talk about it. Saturday, I'll pick it up. You wanna go with? Quit laughing, cabron. Really, I'm busy, cut it out. Bye. **(Hangs up. Walks over to the television, sees the album cover and goes back to the typewriter.)** The Chicano movement had given us several, "plans", "El Plan de San Diego" and "El Plan Espiritu de Aztlán", but the Raza Unida Party would give us organization. It would be a national body, that was both institutional and revolutionary.

So everyone packed and loaded the vans to answer the call. Everyone that is but me.

(Lights come back up on the upper level of the stage.)

Raul

Evelina Móndragon, honor roll graduate, full scholarship to the University of New Mexico, daughter of a New Mexico District Court Judge and a university professor.

Evelina

(Smiling.) Yes?

117

Raul

Evelina Móndragon, who despite her family's well healed connections and the possibility of a full financial scholarship through the University of New Mexico, instead chose to attend this small urban college and work, I repeat work, her way through school.

Evelina

Si Raul?

Raul

Have you decided which van you will be riding in to El Paso?

Evelina

You mean all that way. Thirteen hours on the road, long days and hot nights, packed in a van, tightly together like sardines in a can.

Raul

Yeah, remember I got the tape deck in the dash.

Armando

(In a somewhat matter-of-fact, businesslike and intellectual manner.)

Evelina, don't you think the Central Committee of the organization should ride together? After all you are the secretary.

Raul

Hey wait a minute, Mr. Chairman, I am the vice-chair. Don't you want me to ride in your van?

Armando

You're Vice-Chair, hmm, somehow I had forgotten. **(Smiles and goes back to work.)**

118

Vern

Can you imagine that Squid? Sleeping in a van, in the middle of nowhere, inches from that beautiful. **(is interrupted.)**

Evelina

The community center has lent me their van, the women are all going together. I thought it was important that we used the time to talk about questions that concern La Mujer. **(To Armando.)** Don't you agree?

Armando

Yes, of course, uh, I have some material that you could read.

Raul

(In shock.) All the women? **(Pause.)** all the women?

Vern

What's there to talk about? Women only need to know two things, what to do in the kitchen and what to do between the sheets. **(Laughs loudly but no one else joins him.)** You call it "Women's Lib," I call it "Women's Lip." Did you read my editorial in the paper? You all know that our problems are caused because Mexicans are inherently lazy, it's the Indian blood and a history of non-European work ethics. Therefore, women only to know how to get pregnant, to serve as child bearers, to protect the hearth...**(The phone interrupts the conversation, Oso answers it.)**

Oso

UMAS, yeah, he's right here, **(To Armando.)** El Paso. **(The second phone line rings, Vern answers it.)**

Vern

UMAS, yeah, he's right here. **(To Miguel.)** Your Mom.

(The phone rings down stage, older Miguel goes to answer it.)

Miguel

Hello. Hi mi'ja, **(Pause.)** Hi baby, I'm going to pick you up tonight, Miguelito and Tomas, too. **(Pause.)** Yes, only if they stop being mean to you. Okay, put your Mom on. **(Pause.)** Hi, you want me to pick them up on Sunday? **(Pause.)** No, Luisa, won't be around for the weekend. **(Pause.)** No. She didn't dump me, again. **(Pause.)** Oh, you heard did you? **(Laughs.)** Look. I know you don't like her, but I do. **(Pause)** getting marrie? . I believe that a man should only have one wife. Marriage may not be forever, but the memory definitely is. **(Laughingly changes the subject.)** How's Larry? **(Pause.)** Hang in there, it's much easier to get into a marriage then to get out of one. **(Pause.)** What's wrong with us, Lupe? Did we burn each other so badly that we're determined not to let someone else love us? **(Pause.)** Okay I burned you more than you burned me. Why do I even talk to you? Okay, I'll see you tonight. And tell the boys to lay off Trina, or I'll make them sit through more of my political stories. Yeah, **(Surprised.)** I love you too, good-bye. **(Hangs up.)** Larry must not be around. **(Walks back to the typewriter, sits down, pulls out a cigarette and lights it and goes back to typing.)**

(Scene returns to upstage with students.)

Armando

(On phone.) Okay, call me back when you find out.

Younger Miguel

(On phone.) Okay Mom, I'll come home right after class, good-bye.

Raul

(To Armando.) What's up?

Armando

(Looking serious, tries to shrug it off.) Nothing, just logistical things. **(During this time, more students have crowded the tiny office area, more sleeping bags, duffel bags, an ice chest etc. There are general ad-libs to indicate increased anticipation.)**

Evelina

(**Talking to her van companions.**) I think we need to submit our own manifesto. We can't wait for the men to do it.

Raul

Oh. The men's words aren't good enough for you?

Evelina

It's not a divisive thing, but men have never gone through labor, they've never been single women with kids and you have never looked at a woman as your equal. (**Laughs.**) So how can any man speak for us?

Raul

I have never looked at anyone as my equal. (**General argument, the phone rings. Everyone dives for the phone.**)

Oso

(**Getting to it first.**) UMAS, yeah. (**Hands the phone to Armando.**) It's for you.

Armando

It's for sure then, huh? (**Pause.**) When? (**Pause.**) How did it happen? (**Pause.**) Where were they? (**Pause.**) Sure I see. Thanks for calling. Good-bye. (**Everyone in the room quiets as Armando replaces the receiver, his voice quivers and his eyes blink rapidly unable to focus, He speaks.**) Today in Alamagordo, New Mexico, Ricardo Falcón was shot. (**Struggling to keep his composure.**) He stopped to fill his radiator with water, his car had overheated. The gas station owner claims that he tried to rob him and so he shot Ricardo in the chest. (**At this point some sobbing and gasps rise up, students are questioning, cursing and then become quiet.**)

The police arrested Florencio Granados, who was traveling with Ricardo. He was charged with being an accessory to armed robbery. (**He is reciting as if he is reading a police report.**) They refused to allow Priscilla Falcon to ride in the ambulance with her husband.

(He clears his voice.) Ricardo Falcón died on the way to the hospital. All this took place just hours ago. **(There is a long pause as the words sink in.)**

Older Miguel

(He is writing.) The room was now struck sullen, the air became thick, making it tough to breathe.

(Sobbing is heard from raised stage.)

Evelina moved across the office to the window.

(Evelina does so.)

She opened it to allow a warm summer breeze into the room. **(Miguel stands.)** I did not know Falcon as the others had, so he had not been a flesh and blood person to me. At that age I had no idea of the historic impact this event would have. However, the sense of loss was as though a brother had departed the family. Into this somber moment Vern chose to venture.

(From the raised stage, Vern slowly rises from his seat, near the corner typewriter and walks to the center of the room. He takes a deep breath of air and spits out.)

Vern

Good riddance to bad news.

(Before anyone can react, Evelina lunges into Vern's face, slashing him with her nails. Vern doubles up his fist and hits Evelina squarely in the face. Out of nowhere, Oso steps forward and picks Vern up off his feet.

The force of Vern's retaliation and Oso's intercession had brought the two men to the wall near the open window. Easily Oso holds Vern, head first, out the window. No one moves. They don't want to be drawn into the conflict. The room is completely quiet. Vern begins to whimper, at first crying gently, helplessly. He begs Oso to hold onto him.)

Oso, please don't drop me. Oh God. Please, I don't want to die. You were right, I should keep my mouth shut, oh please God, don't let me go.

122

(Pause.) I will stay away from the office. I was wrong. Don't let me fall.

Older Miguel

I then realized what a sacrifice women and men like Ricardo Falcón make for us. They are willing to forego the only proven level of existence, in order to preserve principle and dignity. They place their lives at risk for an idea. Vern had no principles to die for, he also had none for which to live. Oso released him.

(Oso releases Vern who screams. All the characters freeze with Vern dangling out the window, his eyes bulging out.)

You know there are instants in a person's life that pass, split seconds, that we will question over and over again and never arrive at a satisfactory answer. **(He looks down at invitation for Vern's award, picks it up, uncrumples it and looks at it.)** What the hell was I thinking? **(He laughs and shakes his head, he is now somewhat drunk.)** In that micro-second, that Vern "The Sleaze ball" Gallegos was hanging out the window, suspended between life and death. I dove forward.

(From the raised stage, the younger Miguel dives at Vern, grabbing his military boots, working his way down his body until he is able to steady himself. Vern climbs back in through the window. Everyone in the office, as well as the younger Miguel, is astonished. We hear voices coming from outside the window.)

Voice #1

Hey, there's a man hanging from the window.

Voice #2

Is he gonna jump?

Voice #3

Somebody call the cops.

(A siren is heard, two cops enter the UMAS office, the ugly one asks.)

Ugly Cop

What's going on here?

(Everyone is silent, Vern is on his feet, and kind of slithers out of the room. The younger Miguel steps forward, moving the nearest sleeping bag.)

Younger Miguel

Nothing just packing for a trip, Officer. **(He looks at Evelina across the room. Everything has slowed to a slow motion. He is awestruck by Evelina.)**

Evelina

Gracias **(Pause.)** Carnal.

(Lights down, a drum beats, actors don arms bands and Brown Berets. A slow version of *Yo Soy Chicano* is sung offstage. Actors pose in a parade formation. A man's voice is heard offstage.)

Priest

En el nombre del Padre y el Hijo y del Espiritu Santo...

(Cool wash up down stage.)

Older Miguel

I didn't make the trip to El Paso, but I did go to Falcón's funeral. I wore a black arm band and I think I even cried. Compañero, Ricardo Falcón

All

Presente!

Raul

Chicano!

Armando

Chicano!

Evelina

Chicano!

All

Power!

(All raise fists in the air, lights out on upper level.)

Older Miguel

(Typing.) The irony would haunt me. How a man would rise from a humble campesino background to shake the foundation of the university and state, only to die on the same day as his moral opposite would be given a reprieve. Vern would continue to live and Ricardo Falcon would no longer know that pleasure.

(Lights down, horn honks, voices offstage.)

Trina

'bye Daddy, I love you.

Older Miguel

Te quiero linda.

Boys

Bye Dad, Bye Dad

Older Miguel

Be good for your Mom.

**(Car doors close and car drives off, front door closes. Lights up
and Younger Miguel walks through the door in the dimly lit
living room. He looks around examining the now clean room.
He walks to the stereo and flicks the switch and *Samba Pa Ti* by
Carlos Santana plays. Younger Miguel walks to the desk where
the older Miguel is passed out at the typewriter. Younger
Miguel pulls the sheet out of the typewriter and reads.)**

Younger Miguel

I often sit on the Sunday afternoons with my children, on the weekends
that I have them, and watch the sunset. From my back porch we can
feel it's warmth until it's very last moment on the horizon. I tell stories,
just as my mother and father told me stories, of Pancho Villa and
Emiliano Zapata. I tell them stories of Ricardo Falcon, Cesar Chavez,
Ruben Salazar and Reyes Tijerina. I never mention Vern, or that I saved
his life. I don't think of it that way. Oso was a good man, all I did was
help him maintain his principles.

But the "ex" pulls her car in the alley, the horn blows, the kids grab their
stuff, they kiss me good-bye and run off to their mom's car. They tell
me that they love me and that they are proud to be Chicano.

Back in the house Carlos Santana is playing *Samba Pa Ti*, over and over
again, an all night concert. I sit down at the typewriter and let myself
drift back to Evelina's smile. **(He walks to the phone on the desk,
picks it up and dials a number. After a few moments he places it
at the Older Miguel's ear. They answer hello. Older Miguel
wakes.)**

Older Miguel

Hello? **(Surprised.)** Luisa? What do you want? I didn't call you.
Wait, wait don't hang up. **(In a groggy and drunk tone.)** You know
you're a hypocrite. No wait. I'm a hypocrite too, we all are. None of us
lives up to the principles we say we believe in.

126

Older Miguel

Hello? **(Surprised.)** Luisa? What do you want? I didn't call you. Wait, wait don't hang up. **(In a groggy and drunk tone.)** You know you're a hypocrite. No wait. I'm a hypocrite too, we all are. None of us lives up to the principles we say we believe in.

We can't, but it doesn't mean we shouldn't try. **(Pause.)** Look, I was wrong. I didn't stop to think of anyone's feelings but my own. **(Laughs.)** No, I'm not sorry about peeing in the punch, but about the other thing **(With difficulty.)** about cheating on you. **(Pause, noticing the younger Miguel, who is at the front door getting ready to leave. To the phone.)** Just a second, okay. **(Puts hand over the receiver, to younger Miguel.)** Thanks.

Younger Miguel

You know you're not done yet?

Older Miguel

Yeah, I know.

Younger Miguel

Say, I heard Evelina put on a little weight as she got older.

Older Miguel

You want to know the truth, she always was kind of full figured.

Younger Miguel

She was perfect. **(Pause.)** We all were. **(Smiles, turns to exit, the stops and looks at him.)** Except Vern. **(He exits.)**

(Older Miguel goes back to phone conversation, music up, lights down.)

Fin

El Centro su Teatro: Lantern, lesson giver

A VISITOR to Denver, here as keynote speaker at the recent Colorado League of United Latin American Citizens State Convention, observed affectionately that, "Mexicanos are the only people I know who, in order to celebrate their joy, implore a *Mariachi* to sing sad songs."

"Serafin: Cantos y Lagrimas," the most recent production by Su Teatro, written and directed by Tony Garcia, is not a celebration of happiness. It is raw and sharp-edged with emotion that knifes the soul, stripping away veneer and pretense.

Garcia's writing is uneven — at times being better than good, at other times movingly predictable, creating extremist, almost cardboardy caricatures that annoy. Then they — in the next instant — cause a pained intake of breath, a tightening of the chest — forcing a viewer to squirm in discomfort at a mirrored reflection, frightenly familiar.

Angel Mendez-Soto is Serafin, the tragic protagonist, a Mexicano who is haunted by demons of the past revolution, a life of backbreaking labor. And if not squandered opportunity, then certainly realization that there are junctures — points in a man's life, where the road traveled or unraveled determines the entire course of that life.

Mendez-Soto is brilliant, an actor who need not take a step back to anyone. He is

**TOMAS
ROMERO**

equal to George C. Scott or Dustin Hoffman in their portrayal of Willy L. in "Death of a Salesman." Yes, doubters — he is that good.

Su Teatro offers Chicano theater. If it's tea room comedy and Neil Simon, Noel Coward witticisms you seek, then you should go elsewhere.

It's too early yet in the metamorphosing of writers like Garcia and others. They join him this week in the Bronx in New York for a historic gathering of Latino playwrights.

First must come the catharsis — anguished relief — and release of pent up passion, pain and pathos.

Once the only outlet to rage came with angry bellows and clinched fists. Now pen and ink are the instruments that provide communicating mechanisms for messages of truth.

Chicano writers will chart their own growth, developing themselves as they see fit — but even more importantly as they need to — crafting, crying and, as someone else said, "literally sweating blood" over each word, each line, each play and each story.

The day will come eventually, of course, when light romantic comedy will be written by American Latinos, when humor and uplifting music will replace some of the first expressions of Chicano soul.

And that, too, will be equally as authentic — rich with humanness and spirituality. Not better, but merely different, as Chicano characterizations more fully convey the wide spectrum of earthly experience.

What is important is that what is read, said and written touches, opens you up and makes you feel emotion within.

Su Teatro, at 4724 High St., is a Denver treasure. It is housed in a converted old schoolhouse, with the chalkboards still intact and with only the ghosts and the echoes of children's voices and footsteps remaining inside the structure.

It invites you, almost as someone invites a guest to his home to sip fresh lemonade, coffee, eat cookies or partake of a watermelon slice.

Then you walk into a small, bone-bare room — to fill your heart's cup with insight.

If you listen to the sad songs, then perhaps, when it's time, they'll sing the glad ones.

Tomas Romero, a Colorado native, is active in educational and political affairs.

Review of Serafin; cantos y lagrimas from The Denver Post, July 11, 1990

Picture from Serafin; cantos y lagrimas
Angel Mendez - Soto

Those at birth of Chicano power will find play more meaningful

By Jackie Campbell

The heart of the play *The Day Ricardo Falcon Died* is a look at the Chicano power movement of the 1970s. Those were the glory days of beat-up mimeograph machines, nights in sleeping bags, and vagabond trips in broken-down vans.

As the curtain goes up in Anthony Garcia's play at El Centro Su Teatro, it is the present and we see former Chicano activist Miguel (Rich Beall) trying to make a living as a writer. He rips pages out of the typewriter and tosses them across the room. It is a threadbare cliche. The scene typifies the problems of a first act padded with cliches and sitcom jokes.

When *The Day Ricardo Falcon Died* gets to a second-act flashback in 1972 it sparkles with conviction. It also produces a star in Steve Pacheco as Miguel's younger self, age 16. It is the setups to bad jokes in the first act that lead the play astray.

The flashback to the youthful Chicano movement lights up the stage. At the top of the split-level set, a group of male Chicano activists answer the phones and flirt with pretty Chicanas. They are planning to attend a demonstration when word comes that one of their movement heroes Ricardo Falcon has been shot.

Young Miguel, standing by in fervent admiration, is the one who saves the group from committing a terrible error. It is almost worth the wait for this scene in which everything stops in frozen time and the grown-up Miguel (Beall) remembers.

As a tale of mid-life crisis, *Ricardo Falcon* is only partly successful. As a story about the birth of Chicano power, its message may be most potent for those who were there.

Jackie Campbell is the Rocky Mountain News drama critic.

Review of The Day Ricardo Falón Died

Picture of Ricardo Falcon during an interview shortly before his death

Ludlow, El Grito de las Minas

A Review by Magdalena Gallegos

Ludlow, El Grito de las Minas, (The Cry of the Mines), Written and directed by Anthony J. Garcia, presented by El Centro Su Teatro, through April 20. Assistants to the director Yolanda Ortega Ericksen and Rudy Bustos, music directed by Rodolfo W. Bustos, choreography by Sherry Coca-Candelaria, lighting design by Leo Griep-Ruiz, set design by Joe Craighead, additional Ludlow research by James Ericksen, El Corrido de Enrique Martinez written by Benito Valdez, choreography for Saturday Social by Mollie Chavez.

For Spanish-named persons whose ancestors migrated to Denver from Northern New Mexico, *Ludlow* will spark remembrances of stories told by grandparents whose families worked the coal mines in Southern Colorado on their way to Denver in the early 1900s.

In *Ludlow*, a New Mexican family who has lost their ranch and land to U.S. tax laws, ends up working in the Ludlow coal mines and gets caught in the middle of a strike at the mine and subsequently, a bloody massacre with the U.S. Militia.

Debra Gallegos-Martinez gives a stunning performance in a dual role of Amelia/Sara, a modern day narrow-minded Chicana (Amelia) and her vivacious and spirited grandmother (Sara).

As the play opens, Amelia arrives in Trinidad to dispose of her deceased grandmother's home and belongings. She remembers her grandmother only as a withered old lady who she despised. She would rather be home in Denver taking care of her Anglo attorney husband and son instead of being caught in a winter storm in Trinidad, and forced to spend the night in her grandmothers house. Aaron Lopez, the attorney handling her grandmother's estate matters, is played strongly by Michael Marquez-Harp. He instructs Amelia to read her grandmother's diary which is part of the will. Amelia starts to read the will angrily but soon gets caught up in her grandmother's life. Amelia's tightly knotted bun is let down and she becomes a young vibrant Sara with flowing long hair and spirited personality.

Amelia's life goes fast from a romantic scene on their ranch with her young husband Enrique, played powerfully by Rudy Bustos, to the Ludlow mines where Enrique is killed. Life in Ludlow is hard and the family scenes are touching and filled with joy with the birth of a baby and sadness as the baby dies. There are some wonderful humorous lines which make you laugh and the next minute your heart cries with the tragedy of the sufferings of the miners and their families. The story goes quickly back and forth as Amelia becomes Sara and back to Amelia in her grandmother's house as she becomes acquainted with her grandmother in a different way than she had ever known her.

There is fine acting throughout the play and remarkable singing and music. The flavor of the Southwest stands out in the set design and the folk dances are lively and well executed. Manuel Roybal is wonderful as the feisty older man who fathers a child and shows off like a king rooster in the barnyard. Angel Mendez-Soto as David Montenegro, is the half-Mexican, half-Black union leader who falls in love with Sara after her husband is killed. But their love affair is intentionally sabotaged by Sara's sons who don't want their mother to marry a Black man.

The lighting design shines in a scene that has a remarkable appearance of a real mine. Although this play has Spanish/English dialogue, it is easy to follow even if you do not speak Spanish.

Garcia seems to be doing what August Wilson has done for African-American theater. Garcia is documenting Chicano/Mexicano American history in his continuing saga of original plays. *Ludlow, El Grito de las Minas* is a treat for the heart and spirit.

Ruins from the old mining town of Ludlow where the cast visited in January of 1993

An Obsidian Rain
Legends and Myths Part III
an unproduced film script

Act One
Scene I

(Scene opens in black. We hear the sound of rain falling and a truck struggling to start.)

Narrator

It is a black shiny rain that falls here in Southern Colorado, down from the mountains and into the valley. This morning at 5:00 A.M., the streets reflect head lamps and traffic lights as though one is passing through a mirror. The ground breathes steam, a rising mist that smothers this job-starved town. The pre-dawn traffic heads to work in the strip-mines. They search for the most precious of metals. Gold, a hypnotic ore that meant life and death to the conquering Spaniards who would claim this land for God and King.

Scene II

(Interior of a '55 Ford pickup with the view looking out the windshield. The windshield wipers beat out a pattern of rhythms and squeaks. Rudy Gomez takes a prescription bottle out of the glove box and takes a handful of 'whites.' He tosses the bottle back into the glove box. After several attempts to close the glove box it finally shuts.)

Scene III

(The exterior of the mine gate. The security guard checks Rudy Gomez in.)

Scene IV

(The company locker room. Rudy is changing clothes. His best friend Jake is next to him. Ray, a Chicano in his mid-fifties, approaches Rudy giving him a hard pat on the back.)

Ray

(Only half-joking.) Oyes Rudy, pareces que todavia estás crudo. Hungover? Are you sure you want to work today?

Rudy

(Shrugs Ray's hand hard off his shoulder.)   Just worry about
yourself, Ray. I'll do my job.

(Ray stares Rudy down and walks away.)

Jake

He was just joking, ese.

Rudy

Well, I'm not, Jake. Okay?

Scene IV

(Exterior. Rudy is in the mine underground. Suddenly the
ground rumbles and the shaft caves in. Amid the dust and the
noise two shadowy figures appear and disappear.)

Scene V

(Interior of a crowded cantina, "Louie's Cantina." Rudy and
Jake are standing at the bar drinking.)

Jake

Damn Rudy, how did you get out?   The whole pinche shaft just came
down.

Rudy

Who cares? As you can see, I made it. (Indicates that he is still
alive and real.) I just heard the explosion and the next thing you
know, I'm in the pinche V.P.'s office...(They laugh)...explaining things
to the company lawyer.

Jake

(Seriously.) Tu sabes que, this strip-mining is not right. We are
violating the earth...(Pause.)...and as you can see, it's not too safe.

(People have been periodically coming up to the bar congratulating Rudy on surviving the cave-in. Men pat him on the back and women hug him.

Rudy sees the cigarette smoke fill the mirror behind the bar. He sees a man who looks very Indio. The man looks about 55, is barrel-chested and strong-armed. His hair is long and braided and he wears a hat pulled low across his face. He is walking towards Rudy. Once again the smoke fills the mirror, the Indio is gone and Rudy notices a pretty woman eyeing him.)

Rudy

(Rudy rises to leave. Jake rises to go with him. Rudy calms him.) Why don't you go worry about someone else? Go save the whales. Hell, save the cucarachas. Who cares? I gotta go take a leak.

Scene VI

(Rudy makes a beeline to the woman. Moving through the crowd, he is besieged by well-wishers. He is feeling light headed. Through the window on the bar's front door, he again sees the reflection of the Indio. As the man opens the door, he disappears in the mist and the rain. People in the bar are laughing, they begin to blur and Rudy faints.)

Scene VII

(Interior of Rudy's bedroom in his trailer home. He wakes up, the young woman he saw in the bar from the previous night, is in bed with him.)

Rudy

(Raises his head looks at the woman and groans.) Ugh. (He nudges the woman, sits up and slaps her naked rear end.) Come on, you gotta go. I gotta go to work. (The phone rings. Rudy reaches to answer it. The woman gets up and goes to the bathroom to get dressed.) Yeah. (Although still groggy, he recognizes the voice.) Hi mija. (He lights a cigarette.) No, jita (Exhales) I'm not smoking. No Sonyita, your Papa has to work this weekend. I won't be able to pick you up. (He coughs. The woman is now dressed and leaves without acknowledging Rudy.

137

He sees her also, nonetheless he makes no response.) No, this Saturday can't be your birthday. I'm sorry I forgot. No...No...don't put your Mama on.

(Interior kitchen   Teresa, Rudy's ex-wife, takes the phone from Sonyita.)

Rudy

Hi Teresa, look, they need overtime at the mine. I gotta pay bills, you know. Phone, mortgage...child support.

Teresa

(Sincerely) I heard about your accident. Are you all right?

Rudy

Yeah I'm all right.

Teresa

I was worried you might be hurt.

Rudy

(Cutting in.) and that I might not be able to work.

Teresa

That's not what I meant.

Rudy

What did you mean?

Teresa

(Backing off.) After all you are the kid's father.

Rudy

(Still agitated.) Look, I'll still bring home the paycheck. So you can tell your lawyer to relax. **(Teresa doesn't respond.)** Look I'm all right. I'm not even sore.

138

(Places his hand on his crotch and remembers he is sore.) Tell Sonya I'll come by after work on Saturday.

Teresa

You'll miss the party.

Rudy

(Not letting her get close.) I'll pick her up around seven o'clock and then I'll keep her for a couple of hours.

Teresa

Rudy...**(Hesitates and then changes her mind.)**...your Mom will be here.

Rudy

Good, she can tell you how I'm just like my old man.

Teresa

Fine. Sonya will be ready at seven.

Rudy

(Quickly.) Teresa, I saw him.

Teresa

What? I didn't hear you.

Rudy

Never mind. Good-bye. **(He hangs up.)**

Teresa

'Bye **(She hangs up.)**

139

Scene VIII

(Interior of Estér's kitchen. Estér is Rudy's mother. Seated at the kitchen table are Rudy, Carmen , Rudy's pregnant sister and his brother Felipe. Estér is at the stove flipping tortillas.)

Felipe

Aye Mamá, como me gusta sus tortillas. You are the queen cocinera of the valle. The whole familia together at the dinner table, just like old times, right Rudy?

Carmen

Pos Felipe, everyday at supper must be like old times to you. (Everyone laughs.)

Estér

Gracias a Dios que todavia tengo todos mis hijos aqui, conmigo. (She caresses Rudy's cheek. He shrugs uncomfortably.)

Felipe

(Grabbing a tortilla.) Yeah, I heard you had a close one yesterday.

Rudy

Not really. Not even a scratch on me.

Carmen

(Pouring a glass of water.) Yeah, this time. But what about the next time? (Carmen holds up the glass and looks at the gray water.) And look at this. (Indicates water.) Between the pesticides that they're spraying in the fields and the crap from the strip-mining, we might all be dead soon anyway.

Felipe

I heard gold wasn't the only thing coming out of the mountains. There's talk that some of the metals being dumped in the river are screwing up the water forever.

Rudy

You heard...there's talk...what the hell does that mean?

Felipe

Well you know, I read.

Rudy

Don't tell me you're graduating from high school and you learned how to read too.

Felipe

It happens.

Carmen

(Touching her belly.) I worry about the baby.

Rudy

(Suddenly angry.) Yeah, well why don't you worry about feeding the kid? You guys all bitch about the gold mining and the conditions, but do you ever stop to think that there are no other jobs in this pinche town.

Estér

(Rudy and Carmen start to argue, Estér angrily interrupts.) Callense todos, están en mi casa and what I say goes, got it? Now go on and eat. I cooked all day for you.

Carmen

(Still upset.) Lo siento Mamá, pero I'm not hungry. **(Carmen glares at Rudy as she rises to leave.)**

Rudy

(Between bites.) Where's Beto? It's not like him to miss a meal.

Estér

(Running interference she calms Carmen who returns to her seat.) He went to Alamosa. He heard about a job.

Rudy

(Still baiting.) Did you ever wonder which you enjoy more, the beauty of these picture postcard mountains or the satisfaction of eating three square meals a day.

Carmen

Why are you like this?

Rudy

Because somebody has to work in this family. We can't all live here off Mamá.

Estér

(Firmly.) Rudy, I will say who is welcome in my house. Me entiendes.

Felipe

(Interrupting.) Mamá?

Estér

(Her patience tested.) Yes, Felipe?

Felipe

Can I have the last tortilla?

Estér

(Exhaling.) Si Felipe.

Rudy

I'm going down to Louie's Cantina tonight.

(To Carmen.)

I better not see Beto in there spending money on booze, money that he doesn't have for his family. If he doesn't have money for his pregnant wife, he doesn't have money to drink.

Carmen

(Rising from the table.) Go to hell. I wish to God that you had died in that mine. I hope the mountain opens up and swallows all you assholes.

Estér

(Trying to maintain control.) Mija.

Carmen

(Composing herself.) No Mamá, I'm all right. He can't make me cry like he used to. Rudy, I'm not your weak little sister anymore. Mama, I'll be in my room.

Rudy

(Still eating, but addressed to Carmen.) I better not see him in the bar, or I'll kick his ass all the way home.

Estér

Rudy, nunca supiste cuando hablar y cuando caller. **(She follows after Carmen.)**

Felipe

(Finishing up the food on his plate, he picks it up and takes it to the sink. He rinses it off and places it back on the drying rack.) You gotta take it easy on her. She's seven months gone and the way she and Beto are fighting, you know she ain't getting any. Boy, you two really push each other's buttons. Like I said, 'just like old times.'

Rudy

Que pendejos. Carmen, my sister, the vice-principal and her college professor husband, quit their teaching jobs to move back to a town where there are no jobs and no colleges.

143

Not only that, but they start trying to shut down the only place employing people.

Felipe

Maybe, she believes in what she's doing?

Rudy

So?

Felipe

(Somewhat serious.) So lay off her, huh.

Rudy

(Rising from the table menacingly.) So what are you going to do if I don't?

Felipe

Watch it now I am bigger than you.

Rudy

(Grabbing Felipe) Yeah, but I can still kick your ass. **(Puts Felipe in a headlock.)** You still want some?

Felipe

Yeah I do.

Rudy

(Releases him.) No way man. I gave you some last week. **(Reaching in his pocket.)** You gotta buy your own.

Felipe

(Reaching for the baggie.) C'mon you're always holding. I've got a date. All I want is just a couple of joints.

144

Rudy

(**Relenting.**) Here. (**Handing two joints to Felipe.**)

Felipe

How about a twenty?

Rudy

What? (**Hands it to him. Felipe takes the money and places it in his wallet.**)

Felipe

(**Casually asks.**) What time are you going home?

Rudy

Forget it. Use the back room like I had to. No way, you can't use my place.

Felipe

One more thing.

Rudy

(**Anticipating.**) Get your own rubbers.

Felipe

Thanks.

Rudy

Split.

Estér

(**She enters as Felipe is leaving. Felipe kisses her on the way out. She sits at the kitchen table.**)

Carmen is okay now. She's resting.

                              Rudy

(Begins to leave.) Thanks for supper Mamá. **(Rudy leans in to kiss her and hands her a wad of money. Ester looks at Rudy. He shrugs.)** It's payday. I'll see you later, I'm going to the bar.

                              Estér

Rudy, mijo, I had a dream about you last night.

                              Rudy

Mama, another dream?

                              Estér

No mijo, it was the same dream.

                              Rudy

Come on forget it. You shouldn't eat beans right before you go to bed.

                              Estér

No, you have to listen. I just laid down to take a nap. It was...**(Stops to think.)**...yesterday...**(Stops to think again.)** ...afternoon. I saw your accident. I knew what happened before they called to tell me. He was with you in the mine shaft. Rudy, your Papa is around. He's someplace nearby. I can feel it...

                              Rudy

He's dead.
                              Estér

I never believed it. Rain is not the kind of man to just die and leave everyone in peace.

                              Rudy

Mama, it's been years since you've said his name without saying...

                              146

Estér

(Finishing.) Hijo de la puta madre.

Rudy

Hijo de la puta madre.

Estér

What kind of man leaves his wife and three children alone to fend for themselves? He was never like us. It was the Indian in him, Apache or Yaqui, I don't know.

Rudy

What kind of arrogant fool calls himself Rain?

Estér

Efrain Rodolfo Gomez...it says so on his gravestone. A woman who claimed to be his wife sent me a picture. It was he who called himself Rain. He wanted to name you for him. I made sure everyone called you Rudy so that you would be less like him. (She touches his face, this time he doesn't resist.) Pero mijo, you have his eyes, as black as the mirrored rock you find in the hills.

Rudy

(Reflecting.) Obsidian.

Estér

(Her train of thought interrupted.) Que?

Rudy

The rock is called obsidian. When you break it in half, it reflects. Black...Mysterious...Haunting.

Estér

Rudy, he is nearby. Somewhere.

Rudy

I know Mama, I saw him.

Estér

No mijo, stay clear of him. He only knows how to hurt. After all these years I still miss that hijo de la...

Rudy

(Interrupts.) Okay Mama, I'll be careful.

Scene IX

(Interior of Louie's Cantina, Jake and Rudy are at the bar. They have been at the bar for some time, their words are slurred and their thoughts dimmed.)

Jake

Tomorrow's Saturday. Why are you working?

Rudy

Got to. I need the money...**(Holds up a bottle of beer.)**...To support my habits.

Jake

I can't go in. I've worked eighteen days straight. Besides, it's almost midnight, in five hours I'll still be drunk. **(Jake leans closer to Rudy.)** You know, I've been so tired lately that when I go to bed I don't even have the strength to...**(Pause.)** ...you know...

Rudy

Have sex?

Jake

Have sex? Hell no. I'm too tired to do it to my wife. What makes you think I've got the energy to do it to you.

(Rudy and Jake laugh at Jake's joke.)

Rudy

(Sees Beto, who is talking to people and handing them leaflets about the dangers of the mine.) Beto, you asshole.

Jake

What?

Rudy

My cuñado. My sister is home pregnant and he's out getting drunk. **(Rudy gets off the stool and moves to go after Beto. A heavy hand on his shoulder stops him.)**

Ray

(Turns Rudy around.) Hey Rudy.

Rudy

(Facing him.) What do you want?

Ray

Looks like you've been hitting the bottle pretty hard tonight.

Rudy

Look, I'm off work. I don't have to answer to you.

Ray

If you're hung over, you might have another accident. Just maybe that accident yesterday was no accident. Maybe it was carelessness.

Rudy

Get your fucking hands off me.

Ray

(Grabs Rudy tighter and pulls him closer.) Boy, don't you look at me with those eyes. I know who you are. I know your Daddy. I've got a nice hole in my shoulder from him. On a cold day like this my shoulder gets stiff and I can't help but think of Rain. I've got an ex-wife who's an ex, because your old man took a shine to her. He took her and he didn't even want her. Let's you and me go outside. Hijo de la puta madre. (Rudy breaks loose of Ray's grip and punches him.)

Scene X

(Exterior, behind the bar, in the alley. Ray is beating Rudy to a pulp.)

Ray

Come on cabrón, gimme your best shot. (Rudy swings weakly and grazes Ray's face. Ray responds by hitting Rudy three or four times.) I've been watching you, you're the same type of scum as your old man. You hurt people. You're mad at everyone. (Rudy has fallen to the ground. Ray kicks him.) Now it is time for you to feel hurt. (Ray takes out his knife and approaches Rudy. A figure appears behind Ray who turns around and recognizes him.) Hijo de la puta madre.

Rain

Ramán, after all these years, that's all you have to say to me. (He hits Ray across the face with a 2 x 4.)

Scene XI

(Exterior on a mountainside near the mines. Rain is carrying Rudy, in his arms, up the mountain. It continues to rain.)

Scene XII

(Interior of a mountain cave lit only by a fire. Rudy is shivering under an old army blanket. His face is bruised.)

Rudy

Is this where you live?

Rain

I'm waiting for the interest rates to drop, then I thought I'd sell it and get a bigger place.

Rudy

What the hell do you want?

Rain

Why so much anger towards a man who just saved you from an ass kicking?

Rudy

It was your ass-kicking. Ever since I can remember he's been hounding me. **(Pause.)** He says you slept with his wife.

Rain

Hijo, if I slept with every woman that people accuse me of, I would be a very tired and contented man.

Rudy

So you didn't sleep with her?

Rain

I didn't say that. I said, "If I slept with all the women.....

Rudy

(Interrupting.) Okay, I heard you. And don't call me hijo.

Rain

But you are my son. You are of my seed.

151

Rudy

I'm no more your son because of blood, than my mother was your lover because of sex.

Rain

(Flashing angry.) Wasn't one ass-kicking enough for tonight?

Rudy

Why are you here? What do you want from me?

Rain

I want nothing from you. You have nothing to do with why I am here.

Rudy

(Rejected.) I should have figured as much.

Rain

(Challenging.) But maybe tonight you needed me?

Rudy

(Standing.) You're supposed to be dead. They say you talk to spirits. Is this...(Rudy indicates the cave.)...also part of your mystique?

Rain

Smart mouth, thick skull. There is a lot that you don't know. (He moves to the fire.) Hijo, the rain is heavy and the mountain bleeds because she is being washed away forever. The earth is angry and will not rest until she is satisfied. The greed that scars the land must be punished. Fire will destroy the violators.

Rudy

(Sarcastically.) You sound like a street corner Pentecostal.

Rain

(Painfully.) My son, all my life I have sinned against nature. Taking all and leaving nothing behind. I traveled the world of the four directions. I heard the voices of the eagle, the serpent and the ancient ones. I ignored them. I have sinned against man as well. I stole, I cheated, I killed and I put poison into my body.

Rudy

Why don't you open you own teleministry? You could be rich.

Rain

(Urgently.) Pay attention. I was wrong. This does concern you. It is your life that also hangs in the balance. The rain grows stronger. I stole a father from you, and a husband from your mother. (His tone grows more serious.) There must be a sacrifice to stop the evil.

Rudy

(Amazed.) Old man, you are nuts. You saved my life once, tonight. But you fucked it up for twenty-six years before that. (Rudy vacillating.) Let's say we're even. (Pause.) Then you can leave me the hell alone. (Rudy moves to push his way past Rain and he sees a scar across his neck. Rain's throat has been slit.) What the hell happened there?

Rain

(Matter of factly.) You are rewarded and punished for your deeds in this lifetime, not the next. Three days in a drunk cell, some local farm boys didn't like a longhaired, Mexican-Yaqui-Indian-gambler-thief hanging around, so they slit his throat while the local sheriff watched.

Rudy

Nobody could survive that.

Rain

(Looking directly at Rudy.) I didn't...(Beat.)...save your life only once this week.

Rudy

That was you in the mine shaft.

Rain

No hijo, we are in the mine shaft. **(Rudy looks around and sees that this is true.)** The mine will be destroyed by nature, by the earth. **(The ground begins to shake.)** Fire and water will complete the job. I am the sacrifice.

Rudy

(Scared.) Well, what the hell am I?

Rain

You are my son.

Scene XII

(Interior. Inside the mine shaft which is collapsing. The water is pouring into the mine. Rain has placed himself against a support beam and is trying to dislodge it, exerting all his strength. He barely moves it. Rudy realizes he must make a decision to run or act. Rudy moves to the beam and his force is the difference. The shaft collapses. The mountain swallows the mine, causing the electrical generators to explode and catch fire. The entire mine is collapsing amid sirens, alarms and shouting.)
Scene XIII

(Exterior. On a mountainside, the water from the mountain washes down into the river. Rudy is part of the flush digested. He also flushes into the river. He emerges, gasping for air and splashing about. He manages to stand and wade to shore. Through Rudy's black eyes we look back at the mountain. No one else emerges. The rain continues.)

Scene XIV

(Exterior Along the side of the highway, Rudy walks, as the rain subsides and the sun begins to break.)

154

Scene XV

(Exterior. Teresa's house Teresa answers the door in her nightgown. Rudy hugs her. She doesn't know how to react. After struggling with herself, she puts her arms around him. Rudy collapses and falls to the ground. She cradles him against her chest.)

Scene XVI

(Interior. Rudy kisses her between her partially exposed breasts and turns his head to rest it on her lap. He looks out toward the sun. His black eyes began to mist and then tear. The rising sun is reflected in his eyes.)

Scene XVII

(Exterior. The sun rises brilliantly over the mountains of the San Luis Valley.)

Narrator

There is a peace that emerges when the sun has won it's nightly battle to return warmth to the earth. The azure hummingbird drapes the dawn's brilliant coat across the countryside. It is crowned by Venus, the first and last star in the heavens.

Fin

Ludlow: El Grito de las Minas

Ludlow: El Grito de las Minas
Synopsis

Ludlow... is the story of the 1913, Southern Colorado Coal field strike and the subsequent massacre by the Colorado State Militia of sixteen miners, their wives and their children. Most of the dead were children many of which were Mexicanos. Enrique Martinez, his wife Sara and family were forced to move off their ranchito because of their inability to pay taxes. After Enrique is killed in the mines, in Northern New Mexico, the family settles in Southern Colorado. Two sons, their mother, an uncle and his wife become tenants of in a mining camp owned by John D. Rockefeller.

Amelia Martinez-Thompson is an urban present-day woman who has it all, a husband, a career and a child. She is forced to return to her Southern Colorado roots, when her uncle dies. She returns to settle his affairs and confront the ghost of her Grandmother Sara and her past.

She uncovers a great deal about her grandmother, including an interracial love affair, her own father's involvement in the strike and some things long hidden about herself.

Ludlow: El Grito de las Minas is based on the actual events of the Southern Colorado Coal field Strike of 1914. However all characters are fictional.

Picture from Ludlow: El Grito de Las Minas
Rudy Bustos and Debra Gallegos

Ludlow: El Grito de las Minas
Original run
March 14-May18, 1991
written & directed by Anthony J. Garcia
Assistants to the director-Yolanda Ortega-Ericksen & Rudy Bustos
Music director-Rodolfo W. Bustos
Choreography- Sherry Coca-Candelaria
Lighting Design-Leo Griep-Ruíz
Set Design-Joe Craighead

Saturday Night Social Dance choreographed by Mollie Chavez
La Trajedia de Enrique Martinez by Benito Valdez
For All Our Lives by Anthony J. Garcia

Original Cast

Sara Martinez	Debra Gallegos-Martinez
Amelia Martinez-Thompson	Debra Gallegos-Martinez
Enrique Martinez	Rudy Bustos
David (Negro) Montenegro	Angél Mendez-Soto
Elias Martinez	Manuel Roybál
Aarón Lopez	Michael Marquez -Harp
Jésus Martinez	Paul A. Zámora
Pepe Martinez	Santo Álvarez
Maria Marcucci	Karen G. Slack
Celestina	Susana Córdova
Martha Chapman	Joan Ferris
Alicia Martinez	Caroline Turner

Ludlow: El Grito de las Minas

(Tableau #1. Miners assemble on the stage, opening song.)

Esta cancíon triste
viene de los niños

Levantan sus manos
para unirse en la batalla,

El dia de Abril
pronto en la manana,

Es el dia cuando se pagan
los asesinos

Los niños que murieron
viven para siempre

En las ruinas de las minas
nacio el pueblo nuevo.

(Coro)

Los mineros estaban en huelga
se peliaban en contra de la compania,

En la mañana de Abril venian del norte
Asesinos y matadores
de John D. Rockefeller.

Esta cancíon triste
ya viene de los niños,

Levantan sus manos
para unirse en la batalla.

Miner #1

In September 1913, the miners in coal fields of Southern Colorado, went on strike against the Colorado Fuel and Iron Company. The company was owned by John D. Rockefeller

Miner #2

The miners demanded recognition of their affiliation with the United Mineworkers Union, payment for dead load and the abolition of wages being paid in script.

Miner #3

The miners and their families had been evicted from the company owned housing and were now living in tents provided by the Union. On April 20th in the ninth month of the strike, the Colorado State Militia burned the tent colony at Ludlow to the ground. Nineteen people were killed in the massacre, some were women most of them were children.

Miner #1

Las carpas están quemando!

Miner #2

The tents are on fire!

Miner #3

Oh my God the children!

Miner #1

Aye Dios, mis hijos.

All

My babies, por favór ayudame, where are my babies, etc...

(The Miner's sings once again)

Está cancíon triste
ya viene de los niños,

Levantan sus manos
para unirse en la batalla.

(Lights down, we are in the living room of an old house in Trinidad. Amelia enters, she is a 37 year-old Chicana who is a married professional and troubled. She enters and looks around the room. She speaks to the house.)

Amelia

Okay, you old crazy lady, you got me here now what do you want? Look at this place, junk all over. There must be a disease that old people get, where they try to hang on to everything they have before they die. They can't take it with them when they die, so maybe they can just stockpile it in their homes. **(She moves to the rocking chair.)** I bet you sat there many nights, rocking, thinking. I remember, as a child, watching you stare and shout commands. **(Assumes posture of Grandmother.)** My God you terrified me, where are you old lady? Just like this house, memories and dust. **(Amelia once again assumes the pose)** " I Sara Martinez, I Sara Martinez, I Sara Martinez," like a mantra, a wall protecting you. Through glassy eyes you would focus, seeing everything but not recognizing anything. Here I was your ten year old grandchild, being forced to kiss your withered old cheeks. Your long straight snow white hair, looking more an Apache queen mother than a miner's wife. " I Sara Martinez, on this 21st Day of April...Yo soy Sara Martinez en este el viente un dia de Abril." Well, Sara Martinez, I am your granddaughter, Amelia Martinez-Thompson, and I am sitting in your chair, in your old rocking chair, in your old house in Trinidad, and I'm not afraid of you and your commands and your crazy dirge. I don't know what you hid behind those sad eyes, but it doesn't bother me anymore. **(Amelia sees the telephone)** Let's see if this thing is connected. **(She dials, it is long distance.)** Hi son, this is Mommie, what are you doing? Where am I? I'm at your great-grandmother Sara's...hito I'm here to take care of some business. You don't remember your great-grandmother Sara because she died a long time ago...yes before you were born. I came back to sell her house...Why? Because I'm the only one in the family who is not dead or crazy. **(Amelia gets angry at her child's inane questions.)**

Tommy, is your dad there?...Because I want to talk to him. Hi Tom, I'm at the house. How does it look? It looks like shit. What do you expect for a house that's pretty much been neglected for the last 20 years? You don't remember my grandmother Sara because she died before I met you.

My mom's brother lived in the house but now since he's dead it's just me. The funeral was last week. We didn't make it. Why me? **(Getting angry at her husband's inane questions.)** Because, there is no one else, Tom, It's just me. **(Tired.)** Everyone else is gone. What? I sound tired? Just homesick, hon. Give Tommy my love. I miss you too. `Bye. **(She hangs up.)** Questions? What do you expect from a lawyer and his son?

(She removes a coffee pot from the top of an old stove, and pours herself a cup. She hears a noise, looks out the window and sees that a car is pulling up. She opens the door and shouts out.)

Amelia

Mr. Lopez. Yes, come in.

(Aarón Lopez enters. He is the real estate agent and general "know-everything" in the town. Amelia becomes somewhat chilled by the brief moments that she has been outside in the cold.)

I was afraid that you might miss me, or that you might drive by, you know, thinking that no one was home. Would you like a cup of coffee? Take the chill out of you? **(She pours him a cup)** My strongest memory of Trinidad was how cold it gets down here. Mr. Lopez, I would like to conclude this business as quickly as possible. You did bring the papers? That is why you're here? Someone does want to buy the house? There isn't anything wrong is there?

Aarón

Thank you for the coffee, I'm not chilled. I did bring the papers. That is why I'm here. Someone does want to buy the house and no there is nothing wrong. **(Moves to his briefcase.)**

(**Doesn't necessarily think Aarón is funny. Conceding.**) You're right, Mr. Lopez. I was a bit excited and maybe I do ask too many questions, but I am your client and I expect to be treated with respect.

Aarón

Fine, Mrs. Thompson.

Amelia

Martinez.

Aarón

Fine, Mrs. Martinez.

Amelia

Martinez-Thompson.

Aarón

Fine. Mrs. Martinez-Thompson

Amelia

Amelia. (**Amelia reaches to shake his hand**)

Aarón

Amelia. (**Aaron acknowledges her conciliation**)

Amelia

(**Looking at his business card**) And I'll call you....Aaron.

Aarón

(Correcting her, he pronounces his name with a Spanish inflection)

Aarón.

Amelia

Fine. Can we get on with this business? I was hoping that I could make it back home tonight. I didn't want to spend the night here.

Aarón

Home?

Amelia

Denver.

Aarón

Snowstorm due tonight, you'll never make it past Colorado City. The winds are pretty bad up there. It's not a good place for a girl to travel by herself.

Amelia

Look Aarón, I am not a girl. I am a woman. I am a woman in a hurry. If you would just get your ass moving we could sign the papers and I could get the hell out of here.

(Aarón gives Amelia the papers. While she reads the papers Aarón looks around at the junk scattered around the living room. He thumbs through papers, looks at old newspapers and pictures. He touches the stove and unwittingly he burns himself. Amelia looks up from the papers and then hurriedly signs them. Once she has signed them, he speaks.)

Aarón

You are aware of the stipulations in the will?

Amelia

My grandmother and I were not very close. The only stipulation I know of, was that I needed to come down here and sign the house over in person. I have done that. Now, you can dispose of this junk as you see fit. So good-bye, Aarón, if this girl leaves now she will miss a major storm and the winds in Colorado City. You will shut the stove off for me, won't you?

Aarón

When I was a boy **(Pouring another cup of coffee.)** we would always have "adventures" behind the house here.

We could see your grandmother through the windows. She would watch us but never say anything. Sometime we would make up stories about her being a bruja, a witch. Anyway, I lived in fear of what the inside of this house might hold.

Amelia

Now that you have seen the inside of the house, you can see that it is just an old lady's dump bin. With that bit of nostalgia taken care of, I'm off, and Aaron, if you run into any of your childhood chums, you can tell them that my grandmother was a bruja, a witch.

Aarón

You can't leave.

Amelia

Are you trying to stop me?

Aarón

The papers you signed...

Amelia

What did they say? You tricked me, didn't you? **(Looks at the papers trying to find what she missed)** Look all I came down here to do was to sign away the house. You sell it, use it to pay my uncles medical debts and bang-zoom, me and this girl are out of here. So what did I miss?

Aarón

You are to distribute your grandmother's personal effects.

Amelia

(Relieved that it is not something she has overlooked) Right, I am to distribute her personal effects as indicated in Sara Martinez' diary. Mail me the diary and...better yet, I authorize you to read my grandmother's diary and give away her personal effects as she indicated, and the rest of the junk...burn it. **(Long pause)** So where is this diary?

Aaron

(Aaron opens the briefcase, and hands her a page.) Well, this is the first page **(He looks around at the rest of the room.)** and the rest is ...

(He indicates piles of paper scattered around the room. Aarón turns and exits, not saying anything.

Amelia

(Amelia looks around her and defeated moves to sit on the rocking chair.) You finally got me, you old bitch. I hear you breathing in these walls, I smell your old breath. What do you want? Why did you pick me? You must know how I feel about you. Twenty years dead and you live stronger in this hicksville shanty than you ever did in my memory. You held onto my father until you killed him. When I grew old enough to miss him, what did I have?

You and your wrinkled up face, your white hair and your Apache cheekbones. **(She takes a long breath and begins reading the first page of the diary.)**

I, Sara Martinez, on this 21st day of April 1914, commit to paper the events of my life that have led me to the tent encampment at the Ludlow station. I am 37 years old, yo soy una viuda, a widow. I have two sons that worked the mines for the Colorado Fuel and Iron company. I was borne in the town of Chaperito, in Northern New Mexico, we were not far from Las Vegas, and my father, my husband and his brother worked the merced, a strip of land carried over from the old Spanish Land Grants, it was one of the few land grants that the gringos had not bought up or taken by force. We raised cattle, we shared the land, until taxes we're too high. In 1905 **(The page ends, Amelia looks to the back of the page which is blank.)** In 1905. What happened in 1905. Oh shit, sure, just when you get me interested. You're such a mean old bitch. **(She goes to the piles of paper and begins to looks through them.)**

(Scene switches to the ranchito in New Mexico. Music up, song is the instrumental version of El Grito de las Minas, very manito style.)

Elias

(Calling out) Enrique. **(As no one appears he calls louder)** Enrique!

Enrique

(Enters, putting his shirt on and shushing, Elias.) Shh.

Elias

Chingao mano, it's only three o'clock in the afternoon. Wouldn't it be better to save those kind of things for the night, when the children are sleeping? **(Elias laughs.)**

Enrique

(Quieting him.) Keep it down. Sara is sleeping and I don't want to wake her up.

Elias

Why is it, that she is so tired so early in the day? Or did you keep her up all last night too? **(He laughs again.)**

Sara

(Calling from inside the house.) Quique? Who's there?

Enrique

Nobody. Just Elias.

Sara

Pues, tell your brother to come in.

Enrique

He has to leave.

Elias

(Interrupting.) No I don't.

Enrique

Okay, in a minute. **(Half-whispering.)**

Quick, tell me what you found out and keep your damn voice down. I don't want Sara to hear you.

Elias

Well, I found out that if we don't pay our taxes soon we won't be rancheros for long. The county assessor says that even if we sell our ranchito, that we won't have enough money to pay the taxes.

Enrique

How much do we owe?

Elias

More than $5,000 dollars.

Enrique

(**Shouting.**) Five thousand dollars!

Elias

(**Shushing him now.**) Quiet. Sara will hear.

Enrique

How can we owe five thousand pinche dollars? Doesn't Nayo know that we don't have that much money? I can't believe it. He's our primo. If Tia Florencia were alive she would be rolling over in her grave.

Elias

Quique, our primo is no longer the county assessor.

Enrique

How can that be? He has always been the county assessor.

Elias

I don't know. When I went to Nayo's offices there was a gringo sitting in primo Nayo's desk. He said he was the county assessor and when he looked at our records he said that it showed that we hadn't paid taxes in ten years.

Enrique

That's ridiculous, last year we gave the county two of our fattest cows. I know that they slaughtered them to feed the those poor babosos, imprisoned at the county work farm in Guadalupita.

Elias

The gringo says he doesn't have a record of that, and he wants cash.

Enrique

We've always bartered. Nobody around here carries that much cash.

Elias

Except the gringos.

Enrique

Except the gringos. Elias, if you had such bad news to tell me, why did you come here so happy and make me wait so long to get it out of you?

Elias

Hermano you always figure out the answer to whatever the problem is. I wasn't worried. And then you came out buttoning up your shirt **(Starts to laugh.)** And it was so obvious that you and Sara were ...

Sara

(Sara enters with a pot of coffee and a tray of tortillas and sets them down on the table. She interrupts Elias) I thought that we could eat outside here in the shade. What do think Quique? You will join us Elias?

Elias

I never say no to food.

Sara

(As she sets the table, she continues talking.) So, please finish Elias.

Elias

Mande?

Sara

" It was so obvious that you and Sara were" what?

Elias

Uh, it was so obvious that you and Sara were about to uh...eat. Yeah, it was so obvious that you and Sara were about to eat.

Sara

We don't normally <u>eat</u> at this time, but it was so hot and the children are off performing their chores. Taking a siesta seemed like the thing to do.

Elias

(He is embarrassed.) Good idea.

Enrique

Sara, you can stop, you're embarrassing Elias.

Sara

Am I embarrassing you Elias? You just got married. I'm sure you know that married couples sometimes sleep together.

Elias

Yes, I know that.

Enrique

Okay, let us stop discussing our sleeping habits. Sara has made posole and before the boys get here we can eat like regular gente. Elias, please serve yourself. Sara, come join us.

Sara

(She looks over to the sunset.) I love the ends of afternoons here. The sun cools behind the mountains. I hear the boys fighting as they wash up for dinner. I can tell when you are near, because they quiet as they hear your footsteps.

Enrique

(Changing the subject.) So Elias, I see that married life has not hurt your appetite.

Elias

Nothing could hurt my appetite. I don't know Enrique, Alicia is good cook and a fine companion and all, but I'm so used to being alone and you know, just sitting. Watching the fire or spending all night under a tree tending the herd and looking at the stars. On Sundays, I come up here for dinner or the boys will bring me a plate of chile or some tamales. But mostly, I was alone. It was peaceful. Now Alicia is with me all the time, for breakfast and dinner and even after dinner we sit by the fire and you know, instead of quiet she wants me to make **(Struggles to find the right word.)**

Sara

Out with it Elias, what is this terrible woman doing to you?

Elias

Well she wants conversation.

Sara

Oh my God, you poor man.

Elias

Please don't make fun of me, it is hard for me. At my age, I never thought that I would get married. But here I am, 47 years old, an old man with a child bride.

Enrique

I would hardly call Alicia, a child bride, she is at least as old as Sara. **(Realizing he has put his foot in his mouth.)** But she is probably older, much older. If anyone has a child bride, I have a child-bride. A child bride who is as beautiful today as the day I stole this fragile flower from her well guarded cradle.

Sara

(Glancing at Enrique.) Elias, Alicia is 30 years old. She is not a child. But she is also a woman who was married a long time before her husband, Mario Contreras died. You have always been alone, but when you accepted her as your bride, you asked her to share your life. That is all Alicia wants from you. She wants you to share your life with her. She wants to know what you think about when you look into the fire and when you look up to the stars. Share that with her.

Elias

(To Enrique.) Is this true?

Enrique

(Unsure of how to answer.) Probably? **(Glances at Sara.)** Yes, uh sure.

Elias

And what if you have no thoughts in your head?

Enrique

(Enrique defers to Sara.)

Sara

Then you must tell her how you feel.

Elias

(Drops his head in frustration.) This is impossible, marriage is too difficult. **(Rises and begins to exit.)**

Enrique

(Chasing after him.) Wait. Elias where are you going?

Elias

I am walking home, on the way home. I will think of things to say, at dinner, after dinner and even something to say when I look into the fire. maybe I'll think of something to say when I look up at the stars at night. Thank you Sara and Enrique. May Alicia and I please join you for dinner on Sunday? For all my thinking, I am sure that I will be out of conversation by Sunday.

(Elias exits. Sara looks down and sees the newspaper Elias has left. She picks it up.)

Sara

So what did your primo Nayo have to say about the taxes?

Enrique

Nothing. Why do you ask? **(He turns to Sara, who holds up the newspaper.)**

Sara

Elias, went in to town, yes?

Enrique

Yes.

Sara

So what did Nayo say?

Enrique

Nothing, he's no longer the County Assessor, they replaced him with a gringo.

Sara

So what did the gringo county assessor say?

Enrique

He said that manito rancheros are a dying breed. He said that working land that was your father's and your grandfather's and your grandfather's father's doesn't mean a pinche thing. That you have to live by the rules. Just remember that he can always change the rules. He also said that the Phelps-Dodge mine, in Ratón, has work and that if a ranchero was smart and wanted to feed his family then he should go there and work and send the money home. He said that the manito ranchero should also sell as much cattle as he can afford in order to pay his taxes.

Sara

How long did he say that this would take?

Enrique

Not long. God willing.

(Lights down. Sara removes her apron and steps to the lower level of the stage where she becomes Amelia who is looking through a bundle of papers. Love letters fall onto the floor. Enrique reads from across the stage.)

Enrique

My most precious Sara, tonight I looked into the naked blackness of the sky and saw your face. Suddenly the stars rose up to reflect your eyes, causing shadow to shape the curve of your cheekbones, a present at birth from your Apache grandmother.

I am ever grateful to you for the life that you have given me. Because of you, I can write these words on the pages that will carry my love to you. Because of you. I can read the words that you send me. Yes, I miss making love to you. I miss the, "ends of the afternoon," as you call them. I miss that my son is no longer innocent and that now he works along side me, here in the darkness beneath the earth.

Amelia

(As Amelia..) Whew. This is good stuff. **(Continues reading the letter.)**

It is difficult for a man who has worked in sunlight all his life, to face day upon day, entering the mines in darkness and leaving them well after the sun has left the sky. The money I send you is from the script that I have been able to sell. The company does not pay us in money, so what I send you is what I am able to get, and that sadly is often only fifty cents on the dollar. The three of us, Elias, Pepe and myself share a room with fourteen other miners, so we have all become pretty close. Although the distance and separation have been painful, I thank you for not insisting on traveling with me.

(As Amelia.) Enrique, I'd go anywhere with you. **(Catches herself.)** What am I talking about, this is my grandfather. **(Returns to reading letter.)**

I look forward to seeing you at Christmas. The three of us will leave the mines. If only for a short time we will be a family together.

Elias

(Elias enters with Alícia, Jesus and Pepe who are now grown.) Sara, it does no good to mourn forever. Enrique is dead. I saw the explosion. I spent days on end digging for his body. It was no use. He rests now, Sara, in a mine shaft, deep inside a mountain, somewhere. It is time for us to move on Sara, as a family. The ranchito can no longer feed us. Come Sara, gather your things, we will find a new home.

Sara

(Sara sings softly.)

For all our lives, we've been forced to stand and watch
While the fruit that we created and the sweat that we invested
made him rich.
It's true that he, owns the state, the laws, the wealth
he even owns the land that once was ours.

Oh, the path we've traveled over,
Only reveals where we've been,
The future is yet for us to see.

If the pain is buried in you,
Where no one else will know,
Your secret lies safely here with me.

For all our lives , we have lived each day in pieces
never sleeping for the fear that we might dream.

Is this the way, that it was always meant to be?
Is this the plan God designed for us to live?

Sara

(Sara writes.) When I was a young girl my mother took me to the Catholic Nuns, who provided me with the skills to read and write. I was allowed to read the great books. With my mother's blessing I was being prepared to be an educated bride of Christ. Instead, I became the bride of a ranchero.

Alícia

(Alicia enters, she is sniffling.) We came to Colorado, because there was work in the mines. All there is misery. I hate it here. I want to go back home.

Sara

Alicia, you are not one to complain. What is wrong?

Alícia

I just came back from the dry goods store in Aguilar.

Sara

You know that the company doesn't like the men to buy there. Besides, where did you get money? All the boys bring home is script.

Alícia

I wasn't going to buy anything. I was just going to look.

Sara

Well?

Alícia

It was just as we thought. Everything was much cheaper, and it was better. Overalls there were fifty cents. Here at the company store they cost a dollar and a quarter.

Sara

And that's why you're crying?

Alícia

No, I'm crying, because I'm pregnant.

Sara

Oh my God, Alicia, you're forty years old.

Alícia

Thirty-nine.

Sara

Okay. 39. and how old is Elias?

Alícia

Fifty-six.

Sara

(In astonishment.) Fifty-six. **(Nodding her head in approval.)**
Pretty good. **(Sara laughs.)**

Alícia

It's not funny.

Sara

I'm sorry. Does Elias know?

Alícia

No. And that's what I'm afraid of. What if he isn't happy?

Sara

Are you joking? He will be crowing as if he were the champion rooster
at a cock fight. **(She and Alicia embrace.)**

Alicia

Elias is so hard to figure. He doesn't like to say much so I am never sure
what he is thinking. When I was washing clothes I found this in his
pocket.

Sara

What is it?

Alicia

I don't know. It has writing on it. **(Pause.)** Is it, from **(Pause.)** a woman?

Sara

Would you like me to read it for you?

Alicia

I don't know. I'm afraid. If it's from his lover I don't want to know. **(Closes her eyes.)**

Sara

Alicia, Elias is in the mines 12 hours a day, 7 days a week, and you're pregnant. When would he have time for another woman?

Alicia

Men have ways, Sara. Read.

Sara

(Opens piece of paper and reads.) To all good Union men, the time has come to stand together. The coal field operators have once again refused to negotiate. The United Mines Workers of America, District 15, issues the following seven demands:

1. Recognition of the UMWA as the miner's bargaining agent.
2. Adoption of a union proposed wage scale.
3. An 8 hour work day for all classes of laborers.
4. Payment for dead load.
5. Union selected check weighmen at the mines.
6. Freedom to choose doctors, places of residence, and shopping outlets.
7. Enforcement of and adherence to Colorado mining laws.

Rally 'round the Union boys, the time is near.

(Alicia takes the piece of paper from Sara briskly, folds it, and places it into her pocket. Alicia and Sara exit. The lights dim to show the interior of a cave. Two men are working. One of the men checks the ceiling with his pick to assure that it is solid. The second man is setting up props. They begin to shovel coal into a coal car.)

Negro

Elias Martinez, I am called Negro.

Elias

I know who you are. You are with the union. Look I am an old man. I am not one for causing trouble. Negro if you are a hard worker and a good miner and you help me make money, I will be glad to work with you. If you want to spend the whole day talking union mierda then I will ask the pit boss to give me someone else with whom to work.

Negro

Elias, I asked to work with you because I know that the Mexicanos respect you and you can speak to them.

Elias

Why not you? You're a Mejicano, que no?

Negro

My mama was. My papa was a colored slave who escaped to Mexico. Now you know that no Mexicano is going to listen to me.

Elias

Negro, you've worked in the mines before, I can tell. So you should know enough to save your breath because there isn't that much air down here. Leave me alone or this will be the last time we work together. Me entiendes?

Negro

Si. **(They continue to work loading the coal car. They push it off stage and wait for someone to pick it up. They sit down to take a short break. Negro begins to whistle. Elias gives him a dirty look.)** Hey, I'm a happy type, and besides whistling doesn't take up that much air. **(Elias turns back to work and tries to ignore him. Negro sings.)**

"Cuando fui para las minas, llevaba mi corazon,"

(Elias looks up at him)

I worked the mines in Mexico. While I was there I learned of the international labor movement. One of the miners who worked in the copper mines in Chile taught me this song. It has many names that I don't understand, but I believe in what it says. **(Negro continues song.)**

Cuando vi de los mineros dentro en su habitacion
me dije mejor habita en su concha el caracol.
El minero ya no sabe lo que vale su dolor,
Y arriba quemando el sol"

Elias

(Looking up at Negro.) You sing okay. **(He thinks for a moment.)** How does that go? **(He sings.)** Arriba quemando el sol.

Negro

(Negro sings.) Arriba quemando el sol. **(He speaks.)** You sing the second voice.

(They sing together.) Arriba quemando el sol.

(They laugh. Elias begins to choke. He is having trouble breathing. Negro tries to help him.)

Ándale, hombre let's go up for air.

Elias

No I just need to sit for a bit. I don't want the pit boss to see me like his.

(He rests for a minute. With Negro's help he gets to his feet and continues to work. Lights down. Up on Sara. She sings)

Sara

Arriba quemando el sol,
Arriba quemando el sol,

(She crosses to down stage area and returns to present day as Amelia. She is holding the union's flyer in her hand. She reads)

Amelia

To all good union men. **(She looks at the house.)** What are you trying to tell me? All I can tell is that my abuela Sara Martinez had a tough life and left a messy house. **(Looking out the window.)** Oh shit, here comes that real estate idiot. **(She opens the door before h e knocks.)** What is it, Mr. Lopez? **(Lets him in.)**

Aaron

(Correcting her.) Aaron. **(He smiles.)**

Amelia

What is it?

Aaron

I'm just surprised that your still here?

Amelia

I thought, with the storm blowing in and all that I should wait. You remember the one, with the high winds in Colorado City.

Aaron

Funny thing about storms down here. They sometimes blow in and then they sometimes blow out.

Amelia

Well, this storm didn't even show up, but you did. What do you want?

Aaron

I just wanted to make sure that you were okay.

Amelia

Well, I'm fine. So please go.

Aaron

(Realizes that Amelia suspects that he may have romantic intentions.) Oh, wait a minute. That's not why I'm here. **(He laughs real hard.)** You think that I am trying to put the moves on you? Huh? **(Laughs again.)** I'm sorry but you're just not my type. If you don't mind me saying, you're a lady with a lot of problems. All I want to do is sell a house and get on my way.

Amelia

You knew my grandmother, didn't you?

Aaron

Yeah sure. I was a kid, I played in her yard. Like I said I saw her through the window.

Amelia

No there's more. That's why you consistently try to bait me, isn't it? It has to be because nobody could be that stupid.

Aaron

When I was eight years-old, it was three years before your grandmother died. Me and some of the neighborhood kids were playing in the back. We knew that your uncle Pepe was gone, so one of the kids started throwing rocks at the house. Soon we were all throwing rocks at her house. There were windows being broken but we kept it up. I guess we forgot that she was in there until she came out. Her long white hair waving in the moonlight. We scattered, everyone in a different direction. I stumbled and fell, there, you see at the end of the yard there is a gully and then the arroyo. I lay on the ground certain that I would be murdered by this terrible witch coming toward me. It was as if she were the personification of la llorona.

Amelia

You know, now that you mention it, I had the same terrified image of her.

Aaron

(Trace of a smile.) In that moment as my eight year old life passed before me, she reached down and picked me up onto my feet. She was very strong. I was too scared to struggle. She took me into the back porch. I waited as she went into the kitchen. She came back with a toallita and wiped the dried tears from my face. She bandaged my scraped elbow. Then your Uncle Pepe came home. He drove me to my house and explained to my father what I had done. My father went down on Saturday morning and fixed the windows we had broken. On Saturday afternoon my father gave me the whipping of my life.

Amelia

Well she wasn't as kind to girls. That's a very nice story. Aaron, all that tells me is that you were a juvenile delinquent and your father beat children.

Aaron

You people in the city, you're so quick to categorize people. My father whipped me, and he used a belt. But to this day I remember that whipping, just as I remember the look of pain on your grandmother's face as we called her names and laughed when she couldn't chase after us.

Amelia

Is that why you're hanging around here? You feel guilty for breaking my grandmother's windows? Okay the debt is repaid, all is forgiven, now get the fuck out of here,

Aaron

(Gathers his stuff and begins to exit.) There is a sense of history connected with your grandmother and this house. When you leave that will be broken. They will tear down the house build an apartment complex and she will be gone. **(He exits)**

Amelia

He sure is a lousy real estate agent. **(Telephone rings and Amelia answers it.)** Hello? **(Surprised.)** Hi Tom, No I'm not surprised that it was you. I'm just surprised this old phone can still ring. How's your big case going? Yeah I know that I should be there but this is going to take longer. Not long. Tom, I've been on business trips that have lasted longer than this. What's the big deal? I know I promised that I would be around for you more. Yes, I want to make it work too. I love you too, but don't give me ultimatums. **(Amelia slams the phone down and exits.)**

(Scene changes to the mining camp. Alicia is washing clothes outside the company owned shanty. Elias returns home and has brought Negro with him. Alicia looks up. At first, she is happy to see him but then seeing the stranger she retreats to her washing.)

Elias

Alicia, I'm home. **(He walks over and kisses her on the cheek and then moves over to wash his hands. Negro is doing the same silently. It is obvious that he is not welcome. Pepe and Jesús are not home yet. Sara is in the house cooking.)**

The boys will be coming soon. They were right behind us. Is Sara in the house? **(No answer.)** I guess she is.

Alicia

Elias, can I talk to you?

Elias

Sure.

Alicia

Over here.

Elias

Okay. **(He moves to the side with Alicia.)** What is it?

Alicia

Why did you bring that man here?

Elias

This man is Negro, he ...

Alicia

I know who he is. He's with the Union. Do you want us to get thrown out of this shack. It isn`t much but if the company knows that you are associating with him...how long will you keep your job?

Elias

Who`s to know? I just wanted to offer him a plate of beans. He's a Mexicano and he's alone.

Alicia

We barely have enough beans for us, you could have at least warned me.

189

(She picks up her wash and exits into the house. (Pepe and
Jesus enter. Pepe is 21, Jesús is 14. They enter walking but stop
in mid conversation to acknowledge the stranger.)

Jesús

So how close were you to the getting caught in your own charge? I don't
know, I can hardly wait until I can set charges.

Pepe

Dynamite is dangerous and you gotta know how to handle it. The wrong
spark can set the whole shaft down on you. You know, like the
explosion at the Victor-American mine. Carelessness is what causes the
accidents in the mines.

Jesús

That's not the way I see it. If the operators would wet down the walls as
much as they are supposed to...

Elias

These are my nephews, Pepe and Jesusito.

(The three exchange handshakes. Pepe is hesitant.)

Negro

Pepe, Jesusito.

Jesús

(In a grown up voice, correcting his name.) Jesús.

Elias

This is Negro, he is working as my new partner.

Pepe

I know who he is. What happened to Pietro, the Italiano?

190

Elias

Who cares about the Italiano?   Last time I worked with a Greek, the time before it was a colored guy.
(Pepe and Jesús glance up from washing their hands to look at Negro. Negro smiles.)

You see they must have thought that you were colored. Negro is a Mexicano.

Negro

Well, I am part colored, my Papa was...

Elias

Pero, he's Mexicano too. You know how the pit bosses like to keep all the different nationalities separate inside the mines so we can't speak to each other. To have two Mexicanos working together is a pretty good trick on the company.

Pepe

What are you talking about? He's colored and you're an American.

Jesus

That's not the way the company sees it.

Pepe

Oh yeah, do you get white pay or colored pay?

(Before he can answer, Sara enters stairs to house.)

Sara

(She is in a very good mood.) Buenas noches Elias, buenas tardes mis muchachitos guapos, Pepe. **(She kisses him on the cheek, h e grunts.)** and my little one Jesusito

(She kisses him also. He corrects her.)

Jesús

Jesús.

Sara

(Acknowledging Negro.) And I see we have company.

Negro

Me llamen El Negro, Señora.

Sara

Pos, what kind of a name is Negro?

Negro

Davíd Montenegro, Señora a sus ordines.

Sara

Ahh, encantada. Would you like to join us for supper? Alicia, my sister-in-law, makes the best mole. Have you tasted the red chile we grow in back home in New Mexico? (Notices Alicia is missing.) Elias have you spoken to your wife yet?

Elias

Well I tried, when I first came home she seemed a little upset, then she went off into the house. I don't know what I did.

Sara

Why don't we all go inside, and over supper we can find out just what it is you did.

(They all move to the house except Pepe.)

Are you coming Pepe?

Pepe

Mamá, I don't want to eat with that man.

192

Why, because of his skin color?

That, and I don't need no union trouble. The company gives us work, we have food and they even give us a home.

Sara

Aye, mijo, this is no home. A home belongs to you. I just came from the Trujillo's house. Two of the children have typhus. Why? Because the garbage and the waste and the food all breed disease. They dug a hole beneath the house for us to relieve ourselves, and for privacy we have a burlap sack that covers the opening. No mijo, a home is something that you give your children. This is not the home your papá would want us to have.

Pepe

Papá is dead and this is the best I can do. I work 12 hours in the mines to feed this family. Tio Elias is old. He brings home half as much as I do and Jesus is just a boy. I don't want to hear this colored Mexicano and his Mother Jones rally 'round the union speeches. Things are bad enough, there's no need to make it worse.

Sara

You don't need long conversation around the table. Besides after Alicia makes her announcement, I 'm sure that there will be plenty for us to talk about. Vete mijo, go eat.

(Pepe exits into the house)

El Negro would come around more often. He had gained a foothold among the Mexicanos, through Elias and I suppose through myself as well.

(Negro enters quickly on stage, as if he is looking for someone, he stops suddenly realizing that he is alone with Sara.)

Negro

Oh Señora, disculpe, I was looking for Elias.

Sara

(**Sara challenges him.**)You have some nerve, Davíd Montenegro, calling on a woman when she is all alone. If Pepe were here, he would have to kill you.

Negro

Señora, I meant nothing. I will leave.

Sara

You may sit Davíd, and you may call me Sara. My son will not kill you because we are alone, but it would be a good excuse, as any. By the way, why haven't the coal operators killed you yet? Old Sheriff Jeff Farr in Walsenburg, has been on the CF&I payroll for years and Trinidad's crawling with Baldwin-Felts boys. I hear the United Mine Workers tried to organize here ten years. But you lost.

Negro

That's true, they brought in the Mexicans and Japanese to scab.

Sara

I hear this time they will bring in the coloreds.

Negro

You hear a lot of things, Sara.

Sara

I pay attention and I read. I have a particular interest in that sort of thing. My boys go down those shafts everyday and their lives are the most important things in the world to me. I don't want anything to happen to them. I don't need that type of pain. Is that what you're going to do to me?

194

Negro

Everywhere I have ever been Sara, there have been those who work for the money and those who take the money. The way we live is better than the way the miners live in Mexico and the way the miners live in Mexico is better than the way the miners live in Chile and Africa. About your boys, Señora, the union won't kill them. If I hadn't come along, maybe they'd be free to die trapped in the mine, or shot to death behind some company bar for the few pieces of script he had in his pockets or because he was fighting over some company owned whore. The goons will always be out there Sara.

You say you can read. Well it was the union that first taught me how to sign my name. I would write it and then spend days admiring the shape of my own name. Seeing my name written, showed me that there was a light outside the mines and that there could be one inside the mines as well. If a goon kills one of your boys because he standing up and fighting as a man, it is better than the slow painful death of facing a life in this miserable hell and never knowing that they have value as human beings. I want no harm to come to your boys. I don't want to hurt you Sara Martinez.

Sara

So a strike is coming?

Negro

September 14.

Sara

I hear they already killed one of your men?

Negro

George Lipiatt. Yes, he was a good man.

(Suddenly three men in masks appear from off stage.)

Black Hand #1

Are you the man they call Negro.

195

Black Hand #2

Sure, how many niggers you know speak Mexican.

Black Hand #3

Look I don't want to have to kill you. They said you are a communist
but I said your weren't. Tell them you ain`t a communist and work with
us.

Negro

I have no respect for cowards that hide behind masks. Take them off
and show yourself.

Black Hand #3

Don't insult us, it will only make it worse for yourself.

Negro

Why are you talking to me like this do I know you?

Black Hand #1

We brought the rope, let's string him up.

Black Hand #2

Let's do it quickly before the others get here.

**(They make a move toward Negro who throws them around
pretty easily until one of them manages to get behind him and
he hits Negro in the back of the head. They all begin to beat on
him. Sara appears with a rifle and fires into the air.)**

Sara

Quitanse de el, o les mato cabrones.

Black Hand #2

What did she say?

Black Hand #1

I don't know, but it didn't sound good.

Sara

If you don't let him go now I will kill you. Understand.

(At this point she shoots #3 in the leg. He screams and writhes in pain. The others make a move as if to rush her.)

Sara

Try it, I have five more rounds.

(The Black Hands begin to back off and exit. Elias, Jesusito, and Pepe enter together. They lift Negro to his feet and Jesus and Pepe help him off stage.)

Elias

Sara, we need to prepare, in two days it will be the fourteenth and we will have to leave the company housing. We are moving down the mountain to the field outside Ludlow Station.

(Light down on Sara and Elias)

End of Act One

Ludlow Act II

(Amelia is pacing and glances through the curtains. She appears to be waiting impatiently for someone. Most of the debris has been cleared from the stage. All that is left on the stage is a small stack of papers, the stove and the rocking chair. The rest of the stage, yet unseen, is the tent design. Amelia sees a car pull up. She opens the door to let Aarón in. He enters shaking the snow off and cleaning his boots.)

Aarón

Sorry I'm late, nasty snowstorm kind of crept up on us last night.

Amelia

I thought you were used to the elements in Southern Colorado.

Aarón

I'm sorry Amelia, now I'm the one that's in a hurry. What is it that you wanted?

Amelia

That's twice that you've apologized to me this morning. Is that a record for a lifetime.

Aarón

Amelia, you called me. The last time I was here you told me to get the fuck out of here. Now tell me what it is you wanted to talk to me about so that I can get the fuck out of here.

Amelia

There's no reaching you. Okay, we'll handle it your way. I've loaded up the bulk of her junk, and I will give it to the Catholic Charities. I'm taking the rocking chair, I'm sure my husband will complain. So I was wondering if you had a place for the stove. It's all yours. Call it a bonus.

Aarón

What's that stuff? **(Indicating the pile of papers still in the room.)**

Amelia

The last of the diary. I figured I would go through it this morning. **(Laughs.)** She was a great kidder. You see, that's the joke. There is no diary. One page. One page and then a love letter, a note to herself, a souvenir. All clues and no treasure. Aarón, all this time she dangles the story in front of me. Why should I care about this silly old woman who stayed in this town too long?. **(Catches herself.)** I shouldn't burden you with my problems. Take the stove, you like historical things.

Aarón

You need some help going through the last of her stuff?

Amelia

No it's something I have to do alone. I thought you were in a hurry.

Aarón

Time is a relative thing, tu sabes?

Amelia

No. Thanks anyway.

(Aaron exits. Amelia exits carrying several items out to her car.)

(Music comes up "El Grito de las Minas" and mining couples enter and begin a choreographed dance. The couples are attending a spontaneous party in the tent colony. After the dance is finished, couples exit and Sara enters.)

Sara

The union tent colony became like a family, with people sharing food and hardship. In the beginning, the canvas was late in being shipped from the east. John Lawson, from the Union, says it's because the railroad companies purposely stalled delivery.

Everyone here at the camp seems to speak a different language. It is times like this that I feel fortunate that I can speak both Spanish and English. The union meetings are conducted in seven different languages. Most of the people here are Greek, Italianos, a lot of Mexicanos. Yesterday I met a man, a striker, who said he was from Norway. I guess the cold won't bother him. Well it's not the cold so much as the wind, and the snipers on Water Tank Hill. At night the State Militia shines a searchlight from a spot by the old windmill. If I had a scope for my rifle I'd shoot the damn thing out.

(Pepe enters with Jesús and María, a young girl. Jesús is holding his head. The other two are carrying him.)

Jesusito, what happened? Are you all right?

Pepe

He's okay. It's just a knock on the head. He'll be all right.

Sara

How did your brother get a knock on the head?

Pepe

Let him tell you.

Sara

He's bleeding. You tell me.

Pepe

We went to town this morning.

                                Sara

What the hell were you doing taking your brother into Trinidad?

                                Pepe

(Sheepishly.) We went to Walsenburg.

                                Sara

What the hell are you doing going into Sheriff King Farr's town?
(Sara notices María.) And who are you?

                                María

María Marcucci.

                                Sara

Is your papa here in camp?

                                María

Yes.

                                Sara

Then you better go to him, he's probably worried about you.

                                María

Good-bye Jesús.

                                Jesús

(As if on his deathbed.) Good-bye.

(Pepe rolls his eyes. Sara drops Jesús and goes after Pepe)

Is that what happened? The Sheriff did this? You know he works for the mine operators. He probably gets his checks directly from Rockefeller.

Pepe

It was one of the Baldwin-Felts goons. Pero era la culpa de Jesús.

Jesús

I was just standing on the street corner and he walked up to me and told me that he and the other Baldwin-Felts goons were in town to get rid of all the wops and greasers.

Pepe

Jesús, you were just trying to impress your new wop girlfriend.

Sara

(Interrupting him.) Pepe, shut your mouth, both of you. If I had known that you two were going to grow up to be so stupid, I would not have carried either of you for nine months. If you want to kill yourselves, go lie down in front of one of the trains. Come on, I'll join you. Why would you go into town looking for trouble? Never mind, don't tell me. I have heard enough of your stupidities today. **(To Jesus.)** Can you walk? **(Jesus tries but is having a difficult time. To Pepe.)** Don't just stand there, help your brother. Go inside and stay out of my sight until I calm down. Pepe, you're 21, Jesús is 15, shouldn't the 21 year-old look out for the 15 year-old.

(Elias, Alicia and Negro enter. Alicia is now three months pregnant. She is talking to Elias.)

Alícia

We have to stay here, there is really nothing left for us in New Mexico. It is okay to raise our child as the son of a miner.

Elias

In a tent? What kind of home is that?

Negro

Whether you stay or go, I will respect your decision. What happened to Jesús?

Sara

He had a run in with the a couple of goons from the Baldwin-Felts Agency.

Elias

You see how things have become. How long can we hold out? Let's take the boys and go back home.

Sara

This is our home, it is now for you to make of it what we can.

Elias

I believe in what we are doing too, but this is too much to ask of our familias. I know that the boys will go where we ask them.

Sara

Pepe will stay Elias, as will you. Neither of you likes to be told what to do. You like things to stay the same. Alicia and I are women, we will stay with our families. Jesús, now there's a question, he is always trying to prove himself. He always tries to fix things.

Alicia

Esposo, don't worry about me, the baby or the boys. Make your decision for yourself.

Elias

Well I suppose it could be worse. In some ways it's better than the shacks where the company had us living.

Negro

Yeah and a lot cheaper. I have a stove. It's not much but I think it will help keep the tent warm. Also, we are dividing ourselves into several committees. Those of us who wear the red kerchiefs, like this. **(Ties it around his neck.)** We'll be in charge of providing protection kind of like camp police.

I would like the boys to help build trenches under the tents where we can hide when the sniping starts.

Alícia

Jesús will join you later, he's not feeling too good. I want to check on him. Come Elias.

Elias

Huh? Okay.

Sara

So you must be pretty happy, most of the men have come out with the union.

Negro

Yes, that surprised the company. Surprised me, too. **(They laugh)** You never know until the time comes. Most of the Southern coal fields are shutdown. They have only a handful of scabs coming in. We've able to run them out.

Sara

I hear they brought in coloreds.

Negro

Yeah, and the union coloreds run them off too. Those that get past us become prisoners in the mines. The company guards treat them just as bad as they treated us. Except they ain't got no union to fight for them.

Sara

I hear Governor Ammons is going to send down the Colorado State Militia.

Negro

You sure hear a lot of things, Sara Martinez. Yes, they say they will be here to keep the peace.

Sara

Seems like it will be just another army to back the coal operators.

Negro

You might be right, but if we are smart it won't make much of a difference. So what else do you hear Sara?

Sara

(Pulling out the newspaper.) I hear that the bandit Pancho Villa is scaring the daylights out of the American Military. He's smart and he doesn't want to do what they tell him.

Negro

I know of him from the Mexicanos. They say he's a good man who only kills rich people.

Sara

That's not what the papers say. They say he is as savage as Atilla the Hun. That he's a bloodthirsty murderer, and that they should send troops down to stop him before it is too late. They call it intervention. Some say, it's only time before an incident occurs.

Negro

Like in Cuba. A ship blows up and suddenly the U.S. declares war, sends in troops and Cuba becomes a U.S. Possession. They did it before, they figure they can get away with it again.

Sara

And again. If Mexico is annexed by the United States, how long will it be before the gringos go down there and tell the Mexicanos to go back where they came from? **(They laugh.)**

Negro

Bueno, señora, I must go. As always I enjoy the time we spend together.

Sara

Negro, would you like to call on me sometime?

(Pepe walks out and looks suspiciously at Negro.)

Negro

(Sees Pepe and backs off.) I don't think that would be a good idea señora.

Sara

Davíd Montenegro, you shouldn't let others control your ideas.

(Negro exits.)

Pepe

What was that all about?

Sara

It was about a conversation between two people. Now I have a question for you. What makes you think you can talk to me like that?

Pepe

I don't think it's a good idea for you to be mixing with the coloreds.

Sara

So it was your idea.

Pepe

What?

Sara

You don't like the wops, the Greeks, the unionists or the coloreds. Is there anyone left?

Pepe

The men say that he already spends too much time hanging around here. I just don't want anymore talk.

Sara

Maybe if people would just mind there own business and shut up, there wouldn't be so much talk. **(She storms off angry.)**

Jesús

(Enters with a bandage and a black eye, somewhat groggy) What did you say to make Mama mad this time?

Pepe

(Pepe grabs Jesús and throws him to the ground. He looks at bandaged head of Jesús.) How's your head?

Jesús

It hurts.

Pepe

Well that's too bad because you look stupid, with that thing tied around your head.

Jesús

If I wasn't hurt I'd make you pay. Why are you like this? You were never like this when Papá was alive.

Pepe

Well Papá isn't alive. It's just us you, me, Mamá, Tio Elias and Tia Alicia. No one else, understand? Ever since Papá died we've taken care of her and she's getting older now.

Jesús

Yeah, she's almost 37.

Pepe

And she can't always see when someone is trying to hurt her.

Jesús

Who wants to hurt her?

Pepe

Negro.

Jesús

Negro, don't want to hurt her. He's Tio Elias' friend. He saved his life in the mines.

Pepe

He just did that so that we would go out on strike. Now he knows that if Mamá falls in love with him, she'll make sure that we stay out on strike. Jesús, we can't let Negro hurt Mamá.

María

(Maria appears, timidly, peeking in.) Jesús? I just wanted to see how you were.

Jesús

Hello Maria. (They both look at Pepe)

Pepe

Fine, I'll leave. **(Stops before exiting.)** Jesus how did you ever get to be my brother? Niggers, wops, rednecks.

María

He always seems to be so mean.

Jesús

That's only because he is. Try living with him for 15 years.

Maria

I don't think I would want to.

Jesús

When my papá was alive, he was different. When we lived on the ranchito, he used to show me the best places to fish and where to trap rabbit. We even had a special place to hide from papá. I wished that you could have seen our ranchito.

María

We lived in a small village in Italia. My papá came to America by himself, later on he brought my mamea and mi fratelli y sorrelli. I was the first one born here in America.

Jesús

I was borne in New Mexico, everyone forgets that's in America.

María

Do you want to go for a walk?

Jesús

I'm not really up to walking. Besides how would your Papá feel about you keeping company with a Mexican.

María

I think he would be very angry. But he hates all the boys I like.

Jesús

(Somewhat astonished) You like me?

María

What's wrong Jesús?

Jesús

I feel dizzy.

María

You better sit down.

Jesús

I never had a girl say that she liked me before.

María

Jesús, have you ever kissed a girl before?

Jesús

Well my mamá and my Tia Alicía...but that doesn't count I guess. Have you ever kissed a boy?

María

Yeah, lots of times.

Jesús

What's it like?

María

It's okay. Would you like me to show you?

Jesús

Yeah. **(After much trepidation they kiss.)** Was that okay? For a first kiss, I mean.

María

It was my first kiss, too.

(Lights down.   Telephone rings.)

Amelia

(Amelia enters and answers telephone.) Hello? Tom?! Yes, I am surprised to hear from you?   Well, because I'll be home this afternoon and you knew that. What is it? You lost the case? Which one? <u>The case.</u> You're right, what other case is there? Tom, I'm sorry about the case. I'm sorry that I haven't been there for you and Tommy. And I'm sorry you keep acting like such a jerk. Don't start telling me how you've done everything for me. You're right Tom, without you I'm nothing. Don't forget who worked while you went to law school, Mr. "Three Times to Pass the Bar."

Okay Tom, if you want to leave me, at least wait till I'm there. So that you can walk out. Doing it in my absence kind of loses the effect. Yeah, I'll pick up Tommy at your mothers. **(Tom slams down the receiver. Amelia pulls the receiver away from her ear)** Slamming the receiver in my ear. That's a good effect. **(She pulls a sheet of paper from the pile.)** A birth certificate... Amelia Martinez, January 12, 1914. I never heard of her. **(Amelia looks at the birth certificate more closely.)** Wait a minute, parents Elias and Alícia Martinez.

(Elias, Negro, Pepe and Jesus enter. Elias is crowing like the king of the barnyard. Negro, Pepe and Jesús are celebrating with him.)

Elias

Today, I feel as though I could do the impossible.

Negro

Today, hombre, you have done the impossible.

Jesús

Para Amelia Corazón Martinez, salud y bienvenidos a nuestra familia.

Elias

Today your old viejo Tio Elias, is the proudest cock in the barnyard **(Elias crows.)** Cock-a-doodle-do. Fifty seven years-old and bien macho y cabron. Pepe, my nephew. You are not joining in the celebration. Don't let this old rooster scare you. My crow is worse than my talones. **(Indicates scratching motion and then laughs.)**

Pepe

Sorry Tio, I mean no disrespect, but I think it is a shame that your beautiful daughter was born in such miserable surroundings. **(Before anyone can say anything, there is sniping. They all duck.)** It's coming from water tank hill. It sounds like the machine gun. Let's go.

Negro

(To Jesús) Get the women down below, and tell them to stay low. **(They grab the guns and run off stage. Jesús runs to join the women. The women are in the pit. Celestina, the midwife, talks to Sara.)**

Celestina

This is not a good sign for the child.

Martha

(Excitedly.) It's not a good sign for any of us.

Celestina

Quien es ella?

Sara

La Señora Chapman. **(To Martha Chapman.)** Martha, maybe you can check on my Cuñada Alicia and the baby.

Martha

Dear God, I hope the shooting will end soon. My husband, Mr. Chapman, will be worried, frightened. I am usually at home, come supper time. He'll be waiting. **(She walks toward Alicia.)**

Sara

That's good, go see how Alicía and the baby are doing.

Celestina

La gringa está loca? Si?

Sara

Se me hace que si. Her husband was found dead on the road. They found a note from the Black Hand pinned to his clothes.

Celestina

Sara it is not your lot to take care of the world.

Sara

(**Jokingly.**) What is my future bruja?

Celestina

Quiet. You should have more respect. I have spent many years learning of the healing powers of yerbas and prayer tambíen.

Sara

And love potions and magic spells.

Celestina

Acuerdate, que son regalos de nuestras madres indigenas. When the Spaniards came to Mexico and murdered the holy men, the religion was kept safe with the woman. No God-fearing, Christian man would believe that an Indian woman could have any spiritual power, so they called our power evil. They do it out of fear.

Sara

And you have never sold a love potion, sprinkled salt on a threshold or told the viejitas that you could turn yourself into a lechusa at night.

(**Celestina laughs.**) Everyone needs to eat, including myself. And if my love potion works today, in nine months I can deliver the baby. So maybe I'm just creating future business for myself.

Sara

So what is my future Celestina?

Celestina

La niña está enferma. She can not breathe right. Her lungs are too small. I have anointed her. I have breathed my breath into hers, hoping and praying to give her strength but she is too weak. She will not live.

Sara

(**Shocked.**) Why do you tell me this? Celestina, you are very young to carry the knowledge that you do. The proof is in the callousness in which you present your news. Do not tell Alícia, it will crush her.

Celestina

There is a mountain on the other side of Walsenberg. In the ancient times it was a volcano, full of anger, and fire, and life. Today, it sits alone, quietly alone, the Spaniards called it the orphan, El Huerfano, and they used it to guide their journey. The lonely dead volcano would be a welcoming sign to the lost souls, for which this county is named. Las Animas and el Huerfano, widowed and orphaned. We are those lost souls, the widows and the orphans, in the valley of the purgatory river, el Rio del Purgatorio. Sara Martinez, I did not create these signs. they are all around you.

Sara

Celestina, I am already a widow, that is my past.

Celestina

(**Forcefully.**) Fear for your sons, fear for the Black man that is now a part of your life.

215

I would trade any part of my life, or my sons, or anyone else's so that the child could live.

It cannot be.

The shooting has stopped. We can go upstairs now. Sara, Alícia let me hold the baby. She was so tiny and she seemed to fight for every breath. A frown crossed her face and I could see how determined she was to live.

That's wonderful Martha. **(Sara starts to exit but Martha stops her.)**

Sara, he's gone, isn't he? Mr. Chapman is dead. I saw his body. I didn't want to believe it, but now I know. Thank you, Sara Martinez.

(The women exit. Celestina re-enters.)

The date is January 22, 1914. The women, the wives, mothers and children of the miners, line the streets of La Sagrada Corazón de la Santa Trinidad.

We are one thousand strong. Mother Mary Jones, a longtime organizer for the UMWA, is being held under military arrest, no charges have been filed against her. The number of military arrests numbered 27.

Most of these were union officials. General John Chase was in command of the Colorado National Guard, also known as the State Militia. General

Chase was hardly an impartial peace keeper. His hatred for the Union and the strikers had been shown before in the Northern Coalfield Strike.

Martha

The guard had developed a reputation for drunkenness, robbery, had committed assaults on children and females, and intimidated strikers. One of the guard's favorite pastimes was to have inmates dig their own graves. Some of them went so far as to have the captives write farewell notes to their loved ones. Many of the State Militia were former company guards still receiving salary from the coal mine operators.

Sara

On this day, we will gather at 2:00 P.M. in the downtown streets of Trinidad. We will sing union songs and shout protests, demanding the 82 year-old, Mother Mary Jones, be given due process. Turning down Trinidad's Main Street, we approached the mounted State Militia. They must have felt that we were headed to the San Rafael Hospital, where Mother Jones was being held.

María

As General Chase, pompous atop his horse, pressed against our parade of women, he shouted...

Martha

"Halt". Each one of us despised him, our march came to a standstill and we stared across the row of the State Militia in formation. The General...

María

...brushed against me, and as he did, his spur caught my chest. A pain shot through me and as it did I jerked and the General moved with me, finding himself dismounted, in full view of an audience of jeering women and curbside curiosity seekers.

Alícia

I couldn't help laughing, there was this white, hard military man as vain as Napoleon, a man who had used his position to intimidate and harm the strikers, lying flat on his nalgas.

Celestina

Our laughter soon turned to terror as the General remounted, raised his saber and shouted...

Sara

"Ride down the women"

Celestina

The Cavalry charged three times. General Chase, himself, led the charge, swinging his pistol right and left. The militiamen tore the U.S. flag from our hands. One of our women was slashed across the forehead, another one almost lost her ear.

Alícia

But still we continued to fight. And no matter how General John Chase pretended to ride tall, he would always be shamed. The newspapers would call him,

María

"The great Czar who fell and in fury ordered his troops to trample women."

(Jesús is on stage. He is healed and is whittling. Negro enters and begins a conversation with Jesús.)

Negro

Jesús, I haven't seen you around lately. Not since the little one died. It's a shame that Elias and Alícia have to suffer such a tragedy.

Jesús

Little Amelia never really had a chance. I wish I could have a baby now.

Then I would give it to Tio Elias and Tia Alícia.

Negro

Jesús, you cannot have a baby for somebody else. When you have a child it will be all yours. Just as your family will be all your own to love and take care of. Speaking of that, where is the pretty Italiana that you were seeing?

Jesús

Her Papá don't want her seeing no Mexican, even though he's a miner too. I guess he's right. Everybody should just stick to their own kind. **(He looks up at Negro, indicating he should do the same.)**

Negro

What did Maria say about all of this?

Jesús

It don't matter what she says, it's what I say.

Negro

I bet she says that she don't care what her papá says. Jesús, I know women. María likes you a lot.

Jesús

You know women, huh?

Negro

No, maybe I should take that back. The more you know about women, the less you understand them. But I can tell Maria likes you.

Jesús

Well maybe I just don't want anyone to like me.

Negro

It may be too late, some of us already do. Why are you so angry Jesús?

Jesús

Just look around you, where and how we're living. I have to stop thinking like a boy and start to protect my family like a man.

Sara

(Sara enters carrying a basket of laundry.) Jesús, help me with the laundry **(She notices Negro)** Ahh Señor Montenegro, I haven't seen you in awhile. What brings you out on this windy spring morning?

Negro

(Somewhat embarrassed.) April 20th, It's spring, que no?

Sara

I'm surprised that you notice such things. Does this mean you have also decided to call on me?

Negro

Is that what you hear?

Sara

I hear that the United States has invaded Mexico. That Venusiano Huerta has insulted the U.S. flag, so President Wilson has sent troops down there to protect the Mexicanos from themselves and Pancho Villa. **(They laugh.)**

Negro

What else do you hear?

Sara

I hear that calling Mexicans greasers, on the front page of the Denver Post is very popular and that the country is very anxious to go to war.

I hear that the Governor thinks that things are pretty quiet down here, and that the State Militia has dismantled the Union's Tent Colony at Forbes. Anything else you want to hear?

Negro

(Taken aback.) No that was about all.

Sara

I also hear that you are probably very shy, and sometimes you need pushing.

Negro

You are not the kind of woman that can be pushed.

Sara

Until she is ready.

Negro

Are you ready?

Sara

Yes. (She leans over and kisses Negro then moves away.) Davíd Montenegro, you must speak to my brother-in-law Elias and ask his permission to call on me. After that, you may join us for Sunday dinner. You know there are customs and traditions for a man and a woman.

Negro

Sara, you are not a traditional woman.

Sara

That is not true, Davíd. I enjoy tradition. It is the breaking of those traditions that I enjoy most. (She leans in to hug Negro.)

Jesús

(Jesus enters in a near state of panic.)

The State Militia has begun firing at the camp. We think they killed Louie the Greek.

Negro

Louie Tikas is dead? Show me. **(To Sara.)** Find Alícia and go down below. Let's go Jesús.

Sara

The winds rushed through the Berwind Canyon. For nine months they had whipped across the plain outside of Ludlow where our tent camps were set up. We had withstood all the elements of nature, the wind, the rain and the snow, as December had provided us with the worst snow storm in thirty years. We had withstood the insults, the intimidation, the random shooting and the murdering goons who were now disguised as the Colorado State Militia. But the final combination of fire being fed by men thirsting for blood would bring us closest to our breaking point. By evening on April 20th, the Southern coal fields had become a war zone, as the militia and the miners fought. Having gained the upper hand, the militia began to set the tents on fire. The land had been legally leased by the union, and was indeed the union's property. The militia sought to wipe the striker off the face of the earth. It was not until the next morning that the death toll would be noted.

Pepe

(Enters and sees Jesús lying unconscious.) Jesús, Jesús, please wake up. Talk to me.

Jesús

Pepe, I looked for you all night. Mama, is she all right.

Pepe

Si, and so are Tio Elias and Tia Alicia. We were worried about you. This place is a mess. The fighting has spread from Trinidad to Walsenberg. Where have you been?

Jesús

Negro and I went....

Pepe

Negro, I should have figured. He always brings trouble. That's why were in this mess. Mama was asking about him. Where is he?

Jesús

Pepe, he took me out to Water Tank hill. He wanted to kill the men that were firing from the machine gun.

Pepe

The one they call the Death Special.

Jesús

He said that we should shoot them before they killed anymore of us.

Pepe

Well it wasn't the machine gun that did the most damage, it was the fire, 13 people were found in one of the pits. They were dead. They suffocated.

Jesús

We are family, right Pepe? And we're always going to stick together, right?

Pepe

Of course, we'll stick together. What's wrong Jesús?

Jesús

Well as we got closer to the Death Special, I thought about you and what you said about Negro wanting to hurt Mamá. Pepe, I saw them kissing.

Pepe

So what happened Jesús?

Jesus

I shot Negro, Pepe, he's dead.

Pepe

My God, Jesús, where is he now?

Jesús

We had circled near the mines at Delagua and he fell down the mountain. I couldn't get near him and later on somebody set off charges in that area. I gave up on looking for him. All night long I searched for you. **(He begins to sob.)**

Pepe

Calm down Jesús, no one will ever know.

(Sara enters from behind them she has overheard the story. After a very long pause she moves to Jesús.)

Sara

A mother takes a sacred vow when her child is still in the womb. She takes responsibility for that life and all the actions it takes and all that happens to it. Mijo, are you well enough to stand.

Jesús

Si Mamá.

Sara

The two of you will carry your weapons now and protect every miner, his wife and their children. Too many of us have died and it will now be up to us to ensure that no more harm occurs. Me entienden.

Pepe and Jesús

Si Mamá.

Sara

For the rest of your lives you must remember this moment, and remember what the end of the world looks like. This is where hell meets mortality. It is not only women, children and men that have died here today. It is justice, reason, compassion and humanity that today have gasped their last breath.

(Lights down on Sara, Pepe and Jesús, Sara moves forward removing her Sara garb and once again becoming Amelia. Pepe and Jesús exit.)

Amelia

Sara Martinez, you have taken my father from me twice in one lifetime. You held him from me as a child. He worked the mines to be near you and when I was five he died a miner's death, black lung. Now, you tell me the reason he stayed with you was out of guilt, because he was a murderer. I idolized the memory of a murderer, my father, Jesús Martinez, is a murderer. **(She begins to sob. Aaron enters, the door has been left ajar.)**

Aaron

The door was open I'm glad I caught you. Are you all right? Is there anything I can do? Did I come at a bad time? Would you like me to come back later?

Amelia

I'm all right. There is nothing that you can do. It's not a bad time, because I was just leaving, so you can't come back later.

Aaron

Did you figure out who was supposed to get what?

225

Amelia

Men sure ask a lot of questions you know.

Aaron

Sorry.

Amelia

And apologize, too. Yeah, I know now what she wanted me to have. Everything is taken care of. Now I'm going back home.

Aaron

To Denver, right?

Amelia

That is my home, it is now up to me to make of it what I can.

Aaron

Well since everything is squared away, I guess I don't have any reason to keep you. I have been saving this for the right moment to give you. This must be it. Your Tio Pepe told me that I should place it in your hands, only when everything was settled.

Amelia

Aaron, please don't tease me any more. What is your interest in my family?

Aaron

Down here, we all take a personal interest in each other's lives. Our grandfathers worked those very mines, as did our fathers and ourselves, until they closed. Sara, Jesús and Pepe Martinez fought all their lives, to create the world that they might have envisioned before they left New Mexico. We're a small town. Your grandmother, uncle and father are as much a part of our lives as the Sangre de Cristos and Rio Cuchara Valley.

So when I say good-bye to you, I must also say good-bye to them. **(Aaron stops and looks around the house, one last time he then exits.)**

Amelia

(Amelia opens the letter and begins to read.) A mi querida hija Amelia, Many years ago I made a very big mistake, for which I have caused, my mother Sara and my brother Pepe to suffer much throughout their lives. **(Speaking to herself)** Oh shit, he's going to confess. **(Returns to reading the letter)** Davíd Montenegro was a miner that your grandmother Sara loved. I feared the possibility of them continuing together. Sr. Montenegro was a Mexicano who was also colored, and I feared the pain that might come to my mother because of this. It was on April 20th, a terrible day, one in which many good people died. **(Amelia freezes reading the letter. Negro and Jesús enter.)**

Negro

There it is Jesús, the one they call the "Death Special". It's a machine gun mounted on the back of an automobile. The C.F.&I. made special steel plates for it so that it could fire on the camp. They use it to frighten the miners. They want us to fear them. Are you afraid of them?

Jesús

Right now, I'm afraid of everything.

Negro

Jesús, I'm taking it out. Today is the last time the "Death Special" brings death. **(He turns to leave, three guards appear. Negro doesn't see them. Jesús tackles Negro keeping the guards from seeing him. Negro rolls onto Jesús angrily, not knowing what is going on)** What the hell are you doing ?

Jesús

(Jesús points to the guards.) The guards. They would have seen you.

Negro

(**Smiles.**) Jesús, you saved my life.

Jesús

I didn't mean to.

Negro

Thanks. Now let me up, I have work to do. (**Negro rises and jumps one of the guards, breaking his neck. Jesus knocks the other one out then Negro strangles him. The third has run away. Jesus is dumbfounded by Negro's actions.**) We have to go. The guard recognized me. He will tell the others. I have to leave, don't you see?

Jesús

Yes.

Negro

Don't tell them you saw me. Jesús are you listening to me?

Jesús

Yes.

Negro

Jesús, if they find out, we will both hang for murder. Tell them anything, tell them I died, whatever they will believe. I am leaving. Here is the key to a Post Office Box in the Ludlow Station. When the time comes I will contact your mother.

Jesús

No.

Negro

What?

Jesús

Why do you want to talk to my Mamá?

Negro

Because I love her, Jesús, and I want her to join me wherever I am.

Jesús

I don't want her go with you.

Negro

It will be for your Mamá to decide. Take the key. **(Orders him)** Here. **(Negro places the key in Jesús' pocket. Negro starts to exit)** Jesus when I met you, you were a boy. Today I say good-bye to a man. But remember, a man stands on his own two feet. Good-bye. **(Reaches out his hand to shake hands with Jesús, who still declines.)** Buena suerte, Jesús.

Jesús

(Jesús watches Negro exit. After he exits) Buena suerte, Negro. **(Pause)** I spent that night running, hiding, searching for Mama, Pepe, Tia Alícia or Tio Elias, hoping to find someone. Then before daybreak, something exploded near me. Your Tio Pepe found me. I told him about Negro, me and the "Death Special". Then hoping Negro would not return, I told Pepe that I had killed him. For years, my mother and brother protected my secret. Once I spoke it was too late to change my story. One day I received a letter at the Post Office address that Negro had left for my mother. It was from a friend of his that said only that Negro was killed in a mining accident in Arizona. There was now no means to resurrect Negro, only to have him killed again. **(Jesús begins to age as he moves to Amelia, who is frozen reading the letter)** I write these words to you, knowing that you will not read them until after your Tio Pepe, my mother Sara and I will be gone, and no more harm may come of my sin. With my conscience now at rest, I leave this world with the one regret being that I will not be there to watch you grow, and live and love. Con todo mi amor, your Papa Jesús. **(With the transformation completed, Jesús is now an old man, sickly from Black Lung. He kisses Amelia on the cheek and exits.)**

(Amelia closes the letter, grabs her coat and the last of Sara's papers. She exits the house in Trinidad.)

(Fade to black.)

Sara

(Sara enters.) "I, Sara Martinez, wife of Enrique Martinez and mother of two sons, Pepe and Jesús, commit to words, the passions, hopes, fears and emotions of my life. I am a poor woman, born on a ranchito in New Mexico, come to live the life of a miner's family. On this day, as I view the ashes and misery that man has imposed on man, I see beauty and strength. As I am bent, horribly, as the wind swept piñon trees that line the sides of cañones, still I am not broken. To someday, the child of my child yet unborn, who reads this, I give you what I have, that which is myself. What I am. What I feel. I give you Sara Martinez, your past, arise from these ashes and present yourself, as you are my future.

(Sara returns to her table in Ludlow and begins to write. Lights to black.)

Fin